DAN JENKINS'
TEXAS COLLEGE ✦ FOOTBALL LEGENDS

Doak Walker
MORE THAN A HERO

By Whit Canning

Edited by
Dan Jenkins

SPORTS

IN ASSOCIATION WITH THE
Fort Worth Star-Telegram

WESLEY R. TURNER, President and Publisher
MICHAEL BLACKMON, Vice President, Editorial Director
JACK B. TINSLEY, Vice President, Community Affairs
JIM WITT, Vice President, Executive Editor
KEVIN DALE, Managing Editor

Acknowledgements

All chapters in the "Ten to Remember" section are reprinted
by permission of the *Fort Worth Star-Telegram*. Copyright © 1947, 1948 and 1949
by the *Fort Worth Star-Telegram*. All rights reserved.

Designed by Chris Kozlowski, Richard Epps and Daniel J. Janke

ISBN 1-57028-163-7
ISBN (Leatherbound Edition) 1-57028-175-0

Published by

Masters Press
2647 Waterfront Parkway, East Drive
Indianapolis, Indiana 46214
317-298-5706

For other sports publications in the Masters Press library,
call toll-free 1-800-722-2677 or contact our web site at www.masterspress.com

CONTENTS

Doak and Jenkins: Texas' Finest

In 1995, The Fort Worth Star-Telegram began a bittersweet task. The curtain was coming down on 81 years of Southwest Conference football history and the newspaper set about reliving the glory and the groans for its readers.

It was a grand education for a kid who grew up in Big Eight country. We called the series "Legends of the Southwest Conference" and started with an undersized running back who energized the conference and the country after World War II. Doak Walker, with elastic hips and an insuperable spirit, thrilled college football fans from coast to coast.

His selection in the Dan Jenkins' Texas College Football Legends series was a given. The series will include profiles of a dozen players and coaches who have shaped college football in a state that has been producing Saturday afternoon thrills for decades.

Legendary status is given to one who completes feats that would stagger an average person. Walker's exploits would have staggered several players — and he would probably be embarrassed by the mention.

Playing for SMU in 1945 and 1947-49, Walker was a rare superstar in sports. His skills held no limits: running, passing, blocking, catching or kicking, it did not matter. He also made everyone on the field better — at least those on his team. Those on the other side, however, were often left grasping at air as one of the game's best open-field runners went whizzing by.

Star-Telegram sportswriter Whit Canning said it best: "In a euphoric postwar era that passionately believed in heroes, Walker fit the national self-image like a glove. With a nudge from SMU publicist Lester Jordan, America readily adopted the unpredictable Mustangs, who befuddled opponents with their wide-open, pass-oriented attack, then graciously complimented their victims in a then-customary display of sportsmanship."

Walker's exploits at SMU earned him all-America recognition three times. He won the Heisman Trophy as a junior in 1948. An injury-plagued senior year probably kept him from repeating as the top college player in the land. One of the better testaments to Walker's place in Texas history is the Doak Walker Award, established in 1990 and awarded to the country's top running back. But athleticism is not the sole criteria.

"Well, what I'm really proud of," Walker told Canning in 1995, "is that it isn't just an award they give some guy for gaining a lot of yards. It has to do with a lot of other things — academic standing, citizenship, leadership, sportsmanship — that are much more important."

Simply put, Walker is the kind of sports star we need today. He succeeded at every facet of life through integrity.

Combining talent and integrity is a hallmark of Dan Jenkins. He was hooked on Southwest Conference football as a boy, watching TCU win national championships in the 1930's. As a sportswriter, he figured out someone would pay him to watch the teams he loved. Jenkins' tales of sports stars — fact and fiction — have thrilled fans for four decades.

I tried not to think of the history of Fort Worth sports journalists when I joined The Star-Telegram in 1993, the legacy is unattainable. Jenkins set the standard and his love of Texas football begins here.

Kevin Dale
Managing Editor
Fort Worth Star-Telegram

INTRODUCTION

The Doaker

By Dan Jenkins

P oetry in motion. That's how the old sportswriters used to describe various football immortals. Your Red Grange. Your Don Hutson. Anybody else who came along and made their typewriters hum. But if you applied the phrase to Doak Walker in his heyday at SMU, then you had to say that the only guys who deserved to be in the same backfield with him were Byron, Shelley and Keats.

Doak was that good, all right. However, it also needs to be said that his gridiron poems were the kind that frequently ripped into the hearts of his opponents and made them babble things that didn't rhyme at all.

Magnificent Doak Walker, comma. Dazzling Doak Walker, comma. Amazing Doak Walker, SMU's miracle man, comma.

Things you grew accustomed to reading in those days.

The fact is, no sportswriter's words were worthy of his exploits. And if you were as lucky as I was and got to see him play a few times during those thrilling seasons of '47, '48 and '49. you knew why. Although he weighed only 166 pounds and stood only 5-10, he was quite simply the greatest all-round college football player who ever lived.

Did you hear me? Ever lived.

He ran with the ball — like no one else you've seen,

by the way — threw passes, caught passes, punted, quick-kicked, place-kicked, returned punts and kickoffs, blocked, tackled, intercepted, and there was always the rumor circulating that he not only put air in the ball, but sneaked into a band uniform to play the tuba at halftime.

And doing all that in the red jersey, red helmet, and khaki pants that the Mustangs wore back then, he somehow did it with an alarming gracefulness and a touch of class that hadn't been seen before, and hasn't since.

Graceful, classy Doak Walker, comma.

He also inadvertently hauled the word "peripheral" out of the dictionary.

Excuse me? Peripheral? Could it be operated on?

"Doak Walker runs with peripheral vision." We all read that in more than one newspaper, and read it almost as many times as he nonchalantly sidestepped a defender. I don't recall if it was his coach, Matty Bell, who came

1949 Southern Methodist Offensive Eleven

Doak played for the Detroit Lions for six seasons (1950-55) and earned All-Pro honors four times.

up with the word or whether it was some Texas sports-writer who had a better education than the rest of us.

What it meant was that he seemed to glide in and out of so many enemy tacklers with incredible instinct, he must have had eyes where his sideburns were supposed to be.

Many years later when we were visiting while playing in a golf tournament in Florida, I brought up the word — with a smile.

He smiled back, and said, "I never knew what it meant either. Peripheral. Is that how you say it? I was just tryin' not to get hit."

As the tailback and play-caller on SMU assistant coach Rusty Russell's "Y" formation, an intricate system involving all sorts of sleight-of-hand trickery after it was usually Doak who took the direct snap from center, he became the first three-year consensus all-American from his part of the country, and the only one the Southwest

Conference ever produced.

Doak's Heisman year was '48 when he led SMU to 9-1-1 record, including the Cotton Bowl victory over Norm Van Brocklin and Oregon, but he was even more spectacular in the undefeated season of '47.

In that gliding, zigzagging, peripheral-vision season of '47, he reeled off runs of 96 and 44 yards in the 22-6 win over Santa Clara, 76 and 57 yards in the 35-19 romp over Missouri, 37 yards and then 6 for the only touchdown in the 7-0 win over UCLA, 28 yards in the 14-6 survival with Arkansas, then 76, 61, and 57 yards in the memorable 19-19 tie with TCU.

Most of those were from scrimmage, or after dropping back to pass and finding nobody open, but a few were on kickoff and punt returns.

And none of the above speaks of the touchdowns passes he flipped in the 21-14 win over Oklahoma A&M and

Doak Walker took a shower... ...then he used Vitalis

Doak Walker, former All-American and Detroit Lions' star, led the National Football League in scoring for 1955.

New <u>greaseless</u> way to keep your hair neat all day

"I live in Texas," says football's all-time great, Doak Walker. "I like it—but the hot sun and dry wind are pretty rough on my hair. So are showers. That's why I use Vitalis every day . . . my hair never gets dried out, and Vitalis isn't greasy."

It's as simple as that. Vitalis makes even dry, unruly hair easy to manage. Yet you never have that greasy slickness look because Vitalis contains V-7, the *greaseless* grooming discovery. Along with V-7, Vitalis blends alcohol and other beneficial ingredients to provide superb protection against dried-out hair and scalp—whether they're caused by exposure to water or the great outdoors.

Try new Vitalis with V-7 tomorrow. You'll like it.

New VITALIS® Hair Tonic with V-7®

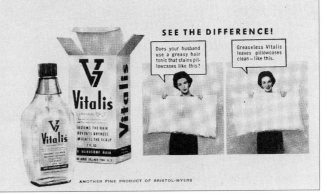

SEE THE DIFFERENCE!

Does your husband use a greasy hair tonic that stains pillowcases like this?

Greaseless Vitalis leaves pillowcases clean—like this.

ANOTHER FINE PRODUCT OF BRISTOL-MYERS

the 13-13 Cotton Bowl tie with Penn State, or his interceptions and other defensive heroics in the 14-0 upset of Rice or the 16-out-of-18 passes that he and Gil Johnson combined to hit in the 13-0 win over Texas A&M or the field goal he booted in the mud to clinch the Baylor game, 10-0, or the towering 53-yard pass he leaped and snagged from Gil Johnson in the 14-13 standing-room-only win over the Texas Longhorns and his good pal Bobby Layne.

That legendary battle with Texas was moved from Ownby Stadium to the larger Cotton Bowl because it matched teams that were undefeated and untied and were ranked that week among the top three in the nation. Texas was No. 2, SMU was No. 3. Small wonder it was the toughest football ticket in the Lone Star state since the SMU-TCU game in Fort Worth in 1935 when the Rose Bowl bid was at stake.

It was one of those games I saw with my own eyes, as they say, and Doak's extra-point was the difference in the end. But that sensational catch of the long pass from Gil Johnson, going high off the ground, barely stretching his fingertips up for the ball, and turning it into the completion which set up the Ponies' second touchdown — and his winning conversion — may have been his greatest single play ever. It was certainly the timeliest.

One more thing about '47. While performing all those feats, and in an era of free substitution, mind you, all he did was average a mere 57 minutes a game, folks.

So he should have won two Heismans, is what I have to say about it.

I can't imagine that anybody has ever had a more impressive football resume. All-district and all-state at Highland Park High, all-conference four years and all-American three years at SMU, All-Pro four out of his six seasons with the Detroit Lions. But along with all that, and perhaps more importantly, Doak is just about the nicest and most modest athlete you would ever hope to meet.

Therefore, I am proud to present him to you now in this book that I hope does him justice.

Doak Walker, Old 37, more than a hero, comma.

THE HOUSE THAT DOAK BUILT: In 1948 and '49, the Cotton Bowl was enlarged twice to accommodate SMU's swelling crowds.

Untamed Mustang

A Quiet Hero Who Led SMU to Greatness

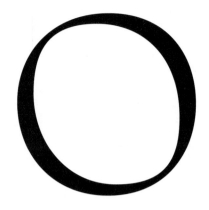n a grim December day in 1949, the SMU Mustangs sat in their dressing room at the Cotton Bowl and listened to a brief, halting speech by a young man wearing an overcoat and leaning on a crutch.

The speaker was Doak Walker, the spangled hero who for three seasons had led them to a succession of thrilling victories, to championships and national acclaim, and into the very hearts and minds of a nation.

Now, on the eve of the biggest game they would ever play — against a legendary juggernaut that had not lost in four years — he had been reduced by injury to the status of spectator. And so, he spoke, in a voice cracking with emotion:

"All my life, I have dreamed of playing against Notre Dame ... now, I can't, but you can. Today, I can't be with you on the field, but you know that I will be with you ..."

Choked up, Walker never finished the speech. But a teammate, the late Johnny Champion, once recalled that had someone not thoughtfully opened the locker room door, the team would have run through it on its way to the field.

A QUIET HERO

The game was a classic in Southwest Conference history. The Fighting Irish preserved a winning streak, a national championship and a 27-20 victory by stopping the Mustangs at the goal line at the end of the game.

It was also to have been the final act of a glittering collegiate career, but it perhaps said more about Walker than all those swivel-hipped runs that left would-be tacklers face down in the grass.

It had long been acknowledged that Walker — the three-time All-American, Heisman Trophy winner, *Life* magazine cover boy — could beat you in any number of ways: running, passing, receiving, kicking, returning kicks, blocking, even playing defense. On the last day of his collegiate career, he proved that he could deal a near-fatal blow to a powerful foe without even suiting up.

But then, it had also long been acknowledged that the personable Mustang star was no mere football player. A year after he left SMU, a book chronicling his superstar feats, *Doak Walker: Three-Time All-American,* was published. In the two decades after its publication, the book was read by nearly every schoolboy in Texas.

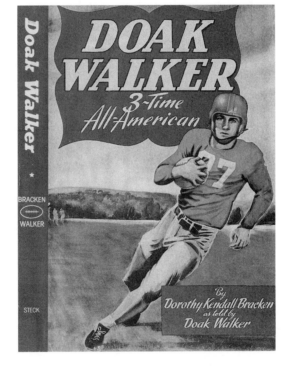

In a euphoric post-war era that passionately believed in heroes, Walker fit the national self-image like a glove. With a nudge from SMU publicist Lester Jordan, America readily adopted the unpredictable Mustangs, who befuddled opponents with their wide-open, pass-oriented attack, then graciously complimented their victims in a then-customary display of sportsmanship.

In particular, fans adopted their leader — the hero whose dazzling skills and indomitable spirit usually carried the day. From the time he teamed with lifelong pal Bobby Layne at Highland Park High School during World War II to his final year with the Detroit Lions in 1955 (again teamed with Layne), Walker was a star who seldom knew failure.

He brought national prominence to a conference that subsequently entered what has sometimes been called a "Golden Era." To accommodate the crowds that came to see Walker, the Mustangs were forced to move from Ownby Stadium on the SMU campus to the Cotton Bowl in downtown Dallas. That stadium was quickly enlarged twice — from 46,000 seats to 75,000 — and came to be known as "The House That Doak Built."

Through the course of those years, Walker built an image that has endured for nearly a half-century. Perhaps in part because of the millions of words used to describe his greatness, none was ever uttered by Walker himself.

"The first thing that comes to my mind about Doak," says his famed SMU teammate, Kyle Rote, "is that he is one of the most decent people I have ever known. I never heard him say anything bad about anyone, friend or foe.

"He was a great team player and an inspiration to everyone around him. And I guess 'I' was the least-used word in his vocabulary."

During his career at SMU — which included the three all-America years of 1947, '48 and '49, plus five games as a freshman in '45 — he accumulated 3,862 yards in total offense and scored 303 points, in addition to another 1,500 yards in kick returns and nearly 500 receiving yards.

He also punted for a 39-yard average and intercepted 12 passes, and his coach, Matty Bell, once said that he could have made all-America as a blocker. He could be shifted among all four positions in the Mustang backfield.

During two injury-free seasons (1947-48), he led SMU to consecutive outright SWC titles and Cotton Bowl appearances and an overall 18-1-3 record.

Although he appeared in only five games as a freshman, he played well enough to be named to the All-SWC team. After spending a year in the service, he came back for three unforgettable seasons.

In the voting for the Heisman in those years, he won the trophy once and finished third twice — including his senior year, when injuries reduced his playing time to a total of 251 minutes.

But Walker's story is not one of statistics or awards. What set him apart and created a legend that has endured half a century was the seeming ability to achieve — by sheer force of will — whatever he wanted to do on a football field.

At 5-11 and 165 pounds, he was considered by many to be too small to play professional football. He not only played, he is now in the Pro Football Hall of Fame.

He never possessed blinding speed — although he had a change-of-pace that could jerk the head off a cobra — yet he won many games by outrunning faster players to the end zone.

His fame lay not in the accumulation of overwhelming statistics but in the eerie ability to somehow rescue a game in the final moments just when all seemed lost.

He was one of the greatest "clutch" players who ever lived, and possessed the true champion's ability to rise to the occasion. Throughout his career, he was unfailingly a "big game" player.

Pinpointing this ability, his great friend and high school and pro teammate Bobby Layne once said, "If you were ahead 28-0, you might as well put him on the bench, because he wouldn't be worth anything. But if it was 7-7, he'd always do something to win the game for you."

This "something" could be literally anything — running, passing, receiving, kicking or returning a kick. He saved one game with an open-field tackle, another with a fumble recovery at the goal line. He won many by simply outsmarting his opponents.

"Having Doak on our team was like having loaded dice or marked cards," a former teammate, Francis Pulattie, once said. "We just felt like we had to do our part and Doak would do the rest. The most amazing thing is that he did it all so effortlessly. He made it look so simple."

A prime example occurred on a soggy, mud-caked field at Baylor in 1947. With the Mustangs locked in a scoreless tie and a drive stalled late in the game, Walker decided that the logical choice was a field goal.

"The goalpost was about 30 yards away, and we were off at an angle," recalls Bob Folsom, later to become the mayor of Dallas. Doak just got Gil Johnson to line up as the holder, like there was nothing to it.

"I was amazed that he actually kicked it, because by that time the ball was so waterlogged and covered with mud, it looked like it would break your foot.

"The whole way, it never rose more than three feet above the crossbar, but he made it. As it turned out, we scored a touchdown a couple of minutes later after an interception, right at the end of the game.

"But that field goal is what won it, and I don't think the idea that he could miss it ever occurred to him."

It was the only field goal Walker kicked in his college career.

"Walker," an unnamed press box denizen once remarked, "has only one specialty — miracles."

Grantland Rice called him, "The most authentic all-around player in football history."

When *Sports Illustrated* put him on its All-Century team in 1969, the press release noted, "Walker did more things well in football, including win ... than just about

> "Nobody ever played football like Doak Walker."
>
> *Matty Bell*

A QUIET HERO

Walker fends off a Longhorn tackler in the SMU-Texas match in 1948.

anyone who ever played."

Matty Bell said simply, "Some called it luck, others called it destiny. But Doak had a natural knack for pulling off great deeds. He was the ideal player and the ideal boy.

"Nobody ever played football like Doak Walker."

One of the greatest influences on Walker's life was Rusty Russell — who coached him (and Layne) in high school and was Bell's offensive coordinator at SMU, and who essentially recruited him for the Mustangs.

In an interview shortly before his death a few years ago, Russell said, "I always had great admiration for Doak Walker. He started out as a little kid playing the game because he loved it, but he always wanted to improve himself and worked at it every day.

"He was never big, about 160 to 165 pounds in college, but when the chips were down you could always depend on him. He was a great leader ... his teammates always felt that if it could be humanly done, he could do it.

"On the field, he could think 15 yards ahead of himself, and he was the greatest there ever was at setting up

LIFE

DOAK WALKER
OF
SOUTHERN
METHODIST

SEPTEMBER 27, 1948 **20** CENTS
YEARLY SUBSCRIPTION $6.00

REG. U. S. PAT. OFF.

A QUIET HERO

Doak joins a trio of Notre Dame all-Americans, (left to right) Emil Sitko, Leon Hart and Bob Williams, in the Irish locker room after their memorable clash at the Cotton Bowl in 1949.

blocks. If you were out in front of Doak Walker, he would make you look like an all-American.

"All those wild things we did at SMU, people always thought we had it planned — but it was just Doak. He ad-libbed, and after awhile, our kids just drifted into the pattern.

"He was an incredible player — and a winner."

In the late 1940's, he also became an American icon. When he and the rest of the Mustangs were featured in a *Life* magazine spread in 1948, they became something akin to America's team. They were young, strong, photogenic, and they won their games in true Hollywood style — in the last reel.

Readers who had held previously no particular affinity for Texans, Methodists, or even football were soon captivated by the young gents of SMU's fling circus. And particularly, their leader.

"There was no one in the world who could match him. No mortal could live up to that much adulation, but Doak Walker did. Lord, how he could play football. He was born to it."

Esquire

As one account put it, some years ago, "Doak was smart, handsome, modest and polite. He went to church and Sunday school. He dated the queen of the campus. His picture was on the cover of *Life* and all the sports magazines.

"If there was such a creature as the all-American boy, Doak was it."

Expanding slightly on the thought, a later account in *Esquire* read, "Doak Walker was everything a football hero should be: handsome, shy, reticent, and unassuming off the field, a cool, swashbuckling brigand on the field. He was every father's shining son, every mother's darling boy, every athlete's sturdy leader, every sorority girl's golden dream.

"There was no one in the world who could match him. No mortal could live up to that much adulation, but Doak Walker did. Lord, how he could play football. He was born to it.

"And when it came time to choose a bride, he married the SMU Homecoming Queen (and Cotton Bowl Queen), Norma Peterson."

The image was cemented with the publication, in 1950, of the *Doak Walker: Three-Time All-American* book by Dorothy Kendall Bracken, one of his professors at SMU.

And it was an image that stuck ... forever.

Through the years, those who were his teammates in Dallas and Detroit have unfailingly referred to him as one of the most outstanding individuals they have ever known.

Those who saw him play at SMU have never forgot-

ten it. It was more than mere skill ... it was as if, somehow, there was magic involved.

And it is notably significant that the last collegiate award he ever won, in 1949, was the Swede Nelson Award — for sportsmanship.

It is an image whose appeal was resurrected 40 years later, in an era of scandal, greed, and a win-at-any-cost mentality.

"Doak Walker epitomized leadership, sportsmanship, and academic and athletic achievement during his storied career at SMU in the late 1940's" states the opening line of the publicity sheet for the Dr Pepper Doak Walker Award, created by the SMU-GTE Athletic Forum and first presented in 1990.

It was established to honor an outstanding running back who also "is in good academic standing, holds a record of good citizenship and leadership, and exhibits the characteristics of sportsmanship and fair play associated with Doak Walker."

Sadly, not all of the recipients have managed to subsequently live up to those standards — but the award remains largely unique in striving to reward achievements beyond the realm of statistical superiority.

"Well," says the namesake, with a flash of the legendary disarming modesty, "I guess one of the best things about it is that they usually wait until after you're dead to do this.

"I feel very proud, and very fortunate."

During a trip to New York City in 1948 to accept the Heisman Trophy, Doak and Norma Peterson took in a pro football game between the Brooklyn Dodgers and the Cleveland Browns.

Doak, Bobby Layne (middle) and Doug McDonald (at center) at Highland Park High practice in 1943.

CHAPTER TWO

A Prodigal at Highland Park High Makes His Mark

In an era of increasingly glitzy football temples adorned with domes, sky boxes and scoreboards that explode like a Normandy beachhead, Ownby Stadium almost looks like something Norman Rockwell painted one day on a corner of Mockingbird Lane.

Most of the homes that face it and fill up the surrounding area have sat there since the century was young. The big Methodist church is still a block down the street. When a planned renovation is completed in a few years, the stadium's seating capacity will rise to 32,000.

But to a small boy growing up in the 1930's, it cast a long, deep shadow.

It was a place of dreams ... home of the famed SMU Mustangs, the only team in Southwest Conference history that had actually played in the Rose Bowl. The place where Bobby Wilson and Harry Shuford had proved that there was football in Texas as good as any in the country.

To athletically inspired youngsters growing up in the comfortable neighborhood around Highland Park High School, it was the center of the universe.

"It was almost like a magical place," says Walker. "As a kid, I always hoped that someday I would play there."

It is one of life's small ironies that as a young man, Walker played so well in Ownby that the Mustangs had to move out of it.

And that a much larger stadium in downtown Dallas that had never figured much in his youthful dreams came to be known as "The House That Doak Built."

He was born Ewell Doak Walker on New Year's Day, 1927, the son of schoolteachers Ewell and Emma Walker. They had met in Sherman, Tex., where Ewell Sr. had attended Austin College and Emma was a local schoolteacher.

After they married and moved to Dallas, Ewell Sr. got a job as a teacher and coach at North Dallas High School. He would eventually become assistant superintendent of the Dallas Independent School District and finally retire after 46 years in the system.

It was a lifetime devoted to helping young people develop the values that would make them good citizens and productive members of the community. And the greatest success he and Emma achieved in that regard was with their own children — Doak, and his younger sister, Pat.

"They were quite a pair," Walker says. "When we were at home at night, she used to play the organ, and he'd pump it.

"My dad taught Sunday school, and on that day you always knew where to find my family. We'd go to the regular church service, then we'd come home and have Sunday dinner, and at night we'd be back in church at vespers. We were also prominent at choir practice."

Although Walker never specifically pushed his son toward football, he certainly wasn't opposed to it. He had played two years in college, and as a coach he regarded it as a healthy athletic pastime and a useful tool for planting certain values in young minds.

"He taught you to be competitive," Doak says, "but he was also very big on sportsmanship, and he stressed it constantly.

"At first, it all seemed to be about football. But as time went by, you began to grasp that he was really talking about something else. The values I have lived my life with, I got from my father, a long time ago."

As for football, a push was hardly necessary. The younger Walker took to it like a duck to a puddle.

And since his father was a coach with the North Dallas Bulldogs, there was ample opportunity for getting oneself involved. It began with Doak playing with the spare equipment stored in a closet in his father's classroom.

There is the story of how, at age 3, he attempted to join a Bulldog scrimmage, but was evicted by his father. By that time, he was drop-kicking a full-sized football over the clothesline in the back yard.

But things definitely stepped up a notch when the family moved into the Highland Park-University Park neighborhood. As Doak grew larger, so did SMU football.

"First we lived on Goodwin, just off Knox, and then we moved to Stanford," he says. "Ownby Stadium was just down the road.

"My dad took me to all the home games, and like any kid I got to where I knew all the players and they were my heroes. In the spring, we used to ride our bicycles up to the school and watch SMU baseball games. It was exciting, and just a perfect way for a kid to grow up."

When the 1935 SMU team swept to 12 consecutive victories and wound up playing in the Rose Bowl, Walker sat in Ownby and watched every home game. He and his father did not make the trip to Fort Worth for the momentous showdown with unbeaten TCU, led by Sam Baugh, but he listened to it on the radio — and exulted when Bobby Wilson caught the pass that beat the Frogs, 20-14.

And although little Bobby was the most famous Mustang, Ewell Walker's son had become fascinated with

THE PRODGAL

Even at the age of 9 months, Doak was headed on a journey to the big time.

another — Harry Shuford, who wore number 37.

"From about 1933 to 1938 my dad was the director of a summer camp up in Colorado," Walker says. "Harry used to come up and help work with the kids, and it was really great. He was a big star with SMU, and I idolized him. Years later, at SMU, I asked for his number."

As the years passed and Walker progressed through grade school and junior high, it became evident that he possessed remarkable skill at the game his father had coached. Just how remarkable, however, was not apparent to all.

Around the time of his induction into the Pro Football Hall of Fame in 1986, Walker was asked in an interview if he could recall one specific moment that had been crucial to the development of his career with SMU and

later with the Detroit Lions.

Perhaps whimsically, he identified a pass he intercepted and ran back for a touchdown in junior high school. His reasoning was that he was playing in the defensive line at the time, and if he hadn't intercepted that pass, "the rest of this might never have happened."

At any rate, watching him zigzag into the end zone, the coach suddenly realized that what he had on his hands was not a defensive lineman.

But the first time the world in general began hearing of Walker was when he reached Highland Park — a remarkable upscale high school in the middle of Dallas that has never been part of the Dallas ISD, where an often amazing level of achievement in all areas has been maintained since before Walker's time.

Continuing with a tradition that began when he was a youngster, Doak tosses a football with his father, Ewell Sr., in the front yard of their Dallas home.

"(My dad) taught you to be competitive, but he was also very big on sportsmanship, and he stressed it constantly. At first, it all seemed to be about football. But as time went by, you began to grasp that he was really talking about something else. The values I have lived my life with, I got from my father, a long time ago."

Doak Walker

It was there that his name began appearing regularly in the local papers. And it was there that he formed two of the most lasting bonds of his life.

One was with a rough, tow-headed youth who lived over on Purdue Street and shared Walker's fiercely competitive spirit. His name was Bobby Layne.

They became renowned as the twin terrors of the Highland Park Scots, then battled as adversaries at Texas and SMU. Reunited with the Lions, they won two NFL titles — and remained best friends until Layne died of cancer in 1986.

In later years, many found it puzzling that the shy, retiring Walker and the garrulous, hard-drinking Layne were close, but for 45 years, the bond never wavered.

"It's true that we were almost opposite personalities," Walker says. "We came from different backgrounds. I had had such a wonderful childhood, and Bobby had a hard life — there had been problems in his family, and he was raised by an aunt and uncle.

"But we were just always great friends, and we also seemed to always provide inspiration for each other when we played together. We always had a feeling, start-ing in high school, that if we played together we could accomplish anything; no one could beat us.

"We were closer than ... probably, we knew each other better than our wives knew us. Through all those years, we never offended each other in any way."

The second great influence on Walker's life that emerged then was the arrival in 1942 of a bespectacled coach with a dozen offenses continually whirling around in his head — H.N. (Rusty) Russell.

Long before he ever reached Highland Park, Russell had gained fame as the coach of the legendary Mighty Mites of Masonic Home — a small, ill-equipped Fort Worth school that had achieved an amazing chronicle of success in the previous decade.

Perpetually confronted by opponents with greater size and squad depth, the Mites had made several stirring charges into the state playoffs using Russell's then-revo-lutionary concept of "spreading the game from sideline to sideline" and then striking through the gaps.

In 1932, the Mites had played a scoreless tie in the state championship game with a Corsicana team led by Bob-by Wilson. In '34, they had beaten Highland Park and lost

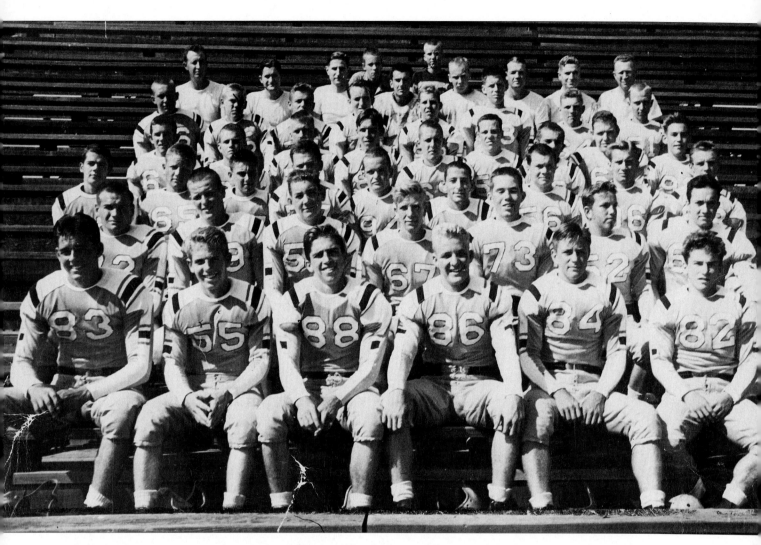

The 1943 Highland Park Scots, which starred Bobby Layne (86) and Doak Walker (84), lost in the state semifinals.

by three points in the semifinals to Blair Cherry's Amarillo team, which won the state championship by a 48-0 count the following week.

The 1938 and '40 teams had both reached the semifinals, and the '41 team — featuring future NFL stars Tex Coulter and Hardy Brown — beat eventual state champion Wichita Falls but was disqualified due to an ineligible player.

All this, Russell had achieved at a school so small that it had to be voted into the Class AA playoffs each time by a special dispensation.

"The first time I ever heard of Rusty," Walker says, "was when Masonic Home knocked Highland Park out

of the playoffs in 1938. They looked ragged, but they sure didn't play that way. The Highland Park fans were so impressed that they bought them new uniforms to wear the next week."

Nevertheless, 1942 was probably Russell's strangest year, since he was the head coach at two different schools — and they almost faced each other in the playoffs.

"That was the weirdest thing I ever saw," Walker says, laughing. "The Highland Park coaches had been inducted into the service, and the school hired Rusty to replace them. But he was still the coach at Masonic Home, and he couldn't get out of the job because the season had already started."

THE PRODIGAL

At the end of the year, Highland Park had won its district and Masonic Home finished in a three-way tie for the title in Fort Worth. The issue was decided by a coin flip — and if Russell had won, he would have had to play himself in bi-district.

Fortunately, he lost — but remained fretful.

"I really hope they think I lost on the up-and-up," he said, "because I really did."

The Scots lost in the quarterfinals to state finalist Sunset, 13-7. They were destined for two strong — but unsuccessful — runs at the state title in 1943 and '44.

In 1943, when Layne was a senior and Walker a junior, they almost made it but were defeated in the semifinals, 21-20, by San Angelo's famed "Angry Orange" team. The Scots seemingly had it in hand with a 20-7 lead, but the Bobcats — one of history's "vow" teams — came back to win that one and the state title game the following week.

With Layne gone to the University of Texas in '44, Walker led the Scots to the title game, but they were beaten by Port Arthur, 20-7.

"During those years at Highland Park, I learned an awful lot of football from Rusty," Walker says. "But I guess more than that, he became kind of a second father to me.

"In fact, we spent nearly as much time over at his house as we did at home. We would go over there after school and go over offenses and formations and concepts until it was time to go home for supper.

"Rusty never tired of it, and he approached it like he was teaching a class. You didn't just get some pointers from him — you absorbed it. Actually, some of his sessions ... ran a little long.

"But it was all a great help to me when I was at SMU, because I knew Rusty's offense like I knew my own name."

When Walker graduated from Highland Park in January 1945, Layne dropped out of Texas and the two pals joined the Merchant Marine. Soon, they were radio operators.

But in October, with the war over and the need for radio operators dwindling rapidly, they were discharged in New Orleans.

That weekend, SMU journeyed to New Orleans to play Tulane, so the boys decided to stay over. The game wasn't much, but there was high subterfuge on a grand scale.

During their time in the service, Layne had convinced Walker that Texas was the place for him.

"He had me talked into it," Walker says, "and we planned to leave after the game so we could be in Austin the next week and enroll. You could do that then, because the schools were still on the trimester system they had used during the war."

Meanwhile, something new had been added at SMU — Matty Bell had hired Russell to run the Mustangs' offense. And when Rusty ran into his two former stars in New Orleans, he invited them to ride back to Dallas with him on the team train.

"We said we'd think about it, and we'd see him after the game," Walker says. "It was a bad game — SMU threw four touchdown passes, but three of them were to Tulane (the Mustangs lost, 19-7) — and afterward Bobby wanted me to go meet Blair Cherry, who was now the Texas backfield coach and was down there scouting SMU.

"We went over to the hotel and rode the elevator up to his room, but he wasn't there. So we decided to go back down and wait for him in the lobby."

As it happened, Cherry had just entered the lobby and stepped into an elevator. As he went up to his room, Layne and Walker passed him going down.

"We were standing around in the lobby, waiting for Cherry (who would succeed Dana X. Bible as Texas' head coach in 1947) to show up," Walker says, "and there were also a lot of SMU people hanging around.

"One of them — a guy I knew who was a big SMU booster — came up and started talking to us, and as he was talking, he kind of maneuvered us around behind one of the columns in the lobby.

"I didn't realize it at the time, but he was keeping us occupied — and out of sight. While he was talking to us, Cherry came down the elevator, walked across the lobby and checked out, and we never saw him.

"Finally, I told Bobby I was going to ride back to Dallas with Rusty because I wanted to see my folks before I went down to Texas. He wanted to stay in New Orleans because his girlfriend (and future wife), Carol, was there. So I said I would see him next week in Austin.

"I caught the train at 8 o'clock and rode back with Rusty and the team, and we got into Dallas about six in the morning. My folks didn't even know I was coming home, so Rusty offered to drive me."

By now, Walker and Russell were happily in the midst of what the current era would deem a recruiting violation. But in 1945, the atmosphere was considerably more relaxed, and the next logical move was breakfast.

"We got to the house and woke everybody up, and

"During those years at Highland Park, I learned an awful lot of football from Rusty. But I guess more than that, he became kind of a second father to me."

Doak Walker

my mom fixed breakfast," Walker says. "And after that, Rusty just kind of hung around, talking with my parents.

"I had a date that afternoon, and we went to a movie. When we got back, Rusty was still there at my house. By the time he finally left, it was dark."

The next morning, Ewell Sr. and Ewell Jr. sat down and discussed the future.

"My dad said, 'Let's look at this logically — where do you plan to live when you get out of college?'" Walker says, "And I said I'd probably live in Dallas.

"He started pointing out the advantages of getting a degree at SMU if I planned to live in Dallas — the friends, business contacts, alumni support — and wound up saying, 'We'd kind of like to have you here with us, and we'd like to see you go to SMU.'"

Besides, if it was good enough for Harry Shuford ...

Highland Park High coach Rusty Russell visits with his three stars, Bobby Layne (86), Doak Walker (84) and Doug McDonald (67).

THE PRODIGAL

"So," Walker says, "I called Bobby and told him I had decided to go to SMU. And he said, 'OK, I'll see you Saturday.' "

Due to the flying-by-the-seat-of-the-pants atmosphere of the moment, Layne and Walker were both able to enroll in their institution of choice, begin classes, draw equipment, get in a couple of days practice, and win a starting position on the varsity by Friday.

Exactly one week after they sat watching a game together in New Orleans, they faced each other as opposing quarterbacks when the Longhorns invaded Ownby on November 3.

Walker drove the underdog Mustangs to an early lead, but Layne led the Longhorns on a late drive climaxed by a touchdown pass to Peppy Blount, and Texas won, 12-7, before a capacity crowd of 23,000.

"Amazing," Walker says. "I still can't believe we did that. It was due to the situation at the time, right after the war, but I imagine it's probably the only time it's ever been done."

The following week, SMU lost to Texas A&M by three points. But after that, with Walker providing the spark on both offense and defense, the Mustangs began to roll. In the final three games they whipped Arkansas, 21-0, and flattened Baylor and TCU by identical 34-0 scores.

Although he played only five games, Walker was named to the All-SWC team after rushing for 289 yards, passing for 387, catching two passes, intercepting two passes, averaging 15.9 yards on 15 punt returns and 23.0 on five kickoff returns, and scoring five touchdowns.

The November surge pushed a struggling SMU team to a 5-6 finish, but Layne had drawn the bigger hand. Losing only to Rice, the Longhorns finished 9-1 and went to the Cotton Bowl.

On New Year's Day 1946, Layne gave one of the most incredible performances in bowl history — completing 11 of 12 passes for two touchdowns, rushing for three touchdowns, kicking four extra points, and capping it by catching a 50-yard pass for a sixth score as the Longhorns

Mr. and Mrs. Ewell D. Walker and their daughter, Patricia, with Doak, at home after he was selected to The Associated Press 1947 all-America team.

Doak was a star outfielder for Highland Park High.

beat Missouri, 40-27.

Afterward, Tiger coach Chauncey Simpson boarded the Texas team bus to personally congratulate Layne for "the greatest performance I have ever seen."

By that time, Walker had been drafted into the Army, and divided the next year of his life between Fort Lewis, Washington, and Fort Sam Houston, in San Antonio.

Without him, the 1946 Mustangs floundered (4-5-1). But '47 was a different story.

CHAPTER THREE

A Star Just Down the Block

When Raleigh Blakely opened a Gulf service station in Dallas in the early 1950's, he figured on the perfect promotional gimmick to get business humming in a hurry.

"We targeted a particular weekend and advertised that Doak Walker would be there all day," he says, laughing. "We had a big blowup of Doak sitting out front, and gave away free 5-by-7's to the customers.

"He was there from eight in the morning 'til eight in the evening, and it looked like all of Dallas stopped by. The next day, we did the same thing with Kyle Rote. We called it the Mustang Service Center and we did real well — but that first weekend was just amazing."

In 1949, SMU's three tri-captains were Walker, Dick McKissack and Bobby Folsom. People often said one of them would be mayor of Dallas someday.

They were right — but they picked the wrong Mustang.

"No, back then nobody ever suggested I was going to be mayor," Folsom says, laughing. "In those days, every eye was on Doak. We were the supporting cast."

Blakely and Folsom — who was mayor from 1976-81 — are yet two more examples of how well Walker's old gang turned out. Each has worked hard and achieved great success in real estate, among other things.

Both have also benefited from their association with a football team that Dallas fell in love with 50 years ago. To have been one of those Mustangs, in Big D, is a badge of honor.

But to Blakely and Folsom, it was mostly just a hell of a lot of fun.

Their careers were similar. Blakely was an end and one of the most prominent receivers in a pass-happy attack. Folsom played end, wingback and defensive back.

They played three years with Doak Walker and finished their careers on the same day — getting banged around by Leon Hart.

In fact, Folsom's career carries an amazing twist — he played either with or against every man who won a Heisman Trophy between 1945 and 1949.

"I was just young enough to miss World War II," he says. "I had a brother, a pilot, who was killed in the war, but I never had to go.

"But I did start out at West Point. My last year in high school (at Sunset), I had a real good season and got recruited by a lot of people, and I had a chance to go up there (Army) so that's what I did. It was 1945, I was 17, and a long way from home."

Sitting out his first year, Folsom in 1946 joined a team that included Dewitt (Tex) Coulter, Barney Poole, Hank Foldberg and Arnold Tucker — each an all-American at some point in his career.

This array was topped, of course, by "Mr. Inside" and "Mr. Outside" — famed back-to-back Heisman winners Felix (Doc) Blanchard and Glenn Davis.

"Needless to say, I was a long way down in the depth chart," Folsom says, "although I did get to play quite a bit

A large crowd of Dallas youngsters gathered to get Doak's autograph at a downtown department store.

A STAR JUST DOWN THE BLOCK

41

"Doak was one of those guys who was just ... amazing. I swear, in practice he couldn't throw the ball 35 yards. Then in a game he'd throw it 50 yards downfield and hit a guy right on the numbers."

Bobby Folsom

because we tended to use a lot of people.

"Pinpointing the highlight of my career up there is easy — when we went into Ann Arbor for a showdown with Michigan. Davis took a pitchout and threw me a touchdown pass in front of 100,000 people, and we eventually won the game, 20-13."

A month later, Folsom found himself sitting in Yankee Stadium watching one of history's most famous showdowns — the scoreless tie between Army and Notre Dame that cost the Cadets a third consecutive national title. On the game's key play, 1947 Heisman winner Johnny Lujack tackled '45 Heisman winner Blanchard in the open field to save the game — and the national title — for the Irish.

"I have to admit," Folsom says, "Lujack made a helluva tackle. It was a pretty big moment — two of the greatest players in history running full speed down the field, head to head."

While at West Point, Folsom witnessed the star-hunger that would later create a nationwide following for Walker.

"Sometimes we would go down and spend the weekend in New York City and go to some of the clubs," he says. "One time several of us went to a movie, and all of a sudden the word started spreading up and down the street that Doc Blanchard and Glenn Davis were in the theater.

"Within minutes there were 5,000 people lined up, trying to get in the movie. The war had ended in '45, and America was hungry for heroes — and that was the era we were in at SMU."

In 1947, Folsom returned to Dallas and enrolled at SMU.

"West Point was great," he says, "but it was a pretty stiff ride both on and off the field. The place was full of all-Americans, and they were all majoring in engineering. Besides, I was the smallest end on the team by 30 pounds.

"But if you want to talk about heroes — I played with Blanchard, Davis and Walker, and you can't get much better than that. Three three-time all-Americans."

They were, however, somewhat different three-time all-Americans.

"With Blanchard and Davis, there was just all this obvious physical ability," Folsom says. "They were both big and fast, with incredible physiques. Blanchard was huge, with great power, and Davis had blinding speed.

"Doak was one of those guys who was just ... amazing. I swear, in practice he couldn't throw the ball 35 yards. Then in a game he'd throw it 50 yards downfield and hit a guy right on the numbers.

"With him, you learned that what really matters is what you do, not how big you are.

"And with us, he was the difference. Probably,

42

except for Doak and Kyle, we were an average team. All we did was win."

But the big thing about Walker the all-American, Folsom says, was who he was, not what he was.

"He got all that publicity, week after week for three years," Folsom says, "and he took it all so well, so modestly. If there was ever any resentment on the team, I never saw it.

"He wasn't a big mixer, but he was friendly with everyone. And they all admired him."

On the gray day when Walker stood, choked, talking to his teammates before they went out to face Notre Dame, Folsom says, the reaction was emotional.

"He just said something about having wanted to play Notre Dame — I can't remember exactly what it was," Folsom says. "But every man on the team reacted to it.

"Because, he was their hero."

And so, Folsom went out like the rest and played like a crazed Viking. And late in the game, he encountered yet another Heisman winner — Hart.

"Last play of my career," he says. "He hit me like a train, and separated my shoulder. My arm was in a sling for six weeks.

"But it was worth it — on that day, and every other. To play with people like Doak and Kyle was more than an honor, it was a pleasure.

"And from the standpoint of living and working the rest of my life in Dallas, it was better than if I'd been an all-American at West Point."

Blakely's recollection of the period is very similar.

"I had been in the service," he says, "and when I got out, I came home and enrolled at SMU. I had started off at Sunset in high school but finished up at Crozier Tech. I had heard of Doak — maybe because his father was the school superintendent — but I has never seen him play.

"I played as a freshman in '46, but we didn't have much of a year. For one thing, the first year after the war I don't think Matty (Bell) really knew how to handle all the war veterans coming back.

"He was one of the greatest motivators I ever saw — really superb at getting a team ready to play — but that first year he was dealing with guys who had just fought a war and they weren't much into the rah-rah stuff."

The next year, everyone adjusted. Plus, there was a new arrival.

"That year," Blakely says, "all I kept hearing was, 'Doak Walker is coming back.' That's about all anybody talked about — including Matty and Rusty (Russell). In fact, all through 1946, the both of them were really planning for the next three years after that. They got together and made plans for it constantly.

"I had a couple of brothers in school, and Matty even told them about it. He said, 'We'll win the championship two of the next three years.' Everybody was that sure about Doak.

"So, I figured this guy must really be a superman. Among the backs we had at the time, the one who came closest to that description physically was McKissack, so when we opened practice, I was lookin' around for some new guy who looked like that.

"When I first saw Doak, I didn't believe it. He was smaller than I was, and I thought, 'What's so great about him?' "

As time passed, however, Blakely made the same discovery that others had about Walker.

"On any day, Monday through Friday," he says, "I could outrun him, outkick him, throw it farther, anything you name.

"On Saturday, I couldn't do any of those things better than he could — and neither could anyone else. When they blew the whistle, he rose to the top.

"He also called the plays, and he was perhaps better at that than anything. Pretty soon we developed the feeling that, 'If Doak called it — it's gonna work.'

"The thing most people remember about him was the way he ran with the ball, but he also called a great game every time and did a great job directing the passing attack.

"This was because he used every play we had, and every receiver. In one year there, I think Kyle had 19 catches and I had 18 and there were three or four guys behind us with 15, 16 or 17. Plus, the defense never knew what he was going to do — or when he was going to do it."

Sometimes, neither did Blakely.

"When we went up and played Pittsburgh," he says, "I was running a certain route where I discovered I could shake free anytime, so I came back and told Doak I was open on what we called a 24 Jump Pass. This was midway through the first quarter, and when I told him, he nodded.

"But we kept going and going, doing other things, and I got irritated, and I thought, 'Dang it, he's not gonna call that play.'

"Finally, it's halfway through the third quarter and we're in the huddle and all of a sudden he says, in that high-pitched voice he had, 'Blakely, where'd you say you'd be on that 24 Jump?'

"It startled me, because by that time I'd forgotten all about it. But we ran it and scored a touchdown."

Many of the seniors who finished up in '49 had been on the '46 team, while others had come in with Walker in '47. Whatever the case, Blakely says, a great transformation occurred during his second year at SMU.

"I guess you could call it chemistry or something," he says, "but the fact is that from '47 on, we were doing a lot of things we were unable to do in '46. In fact, I do believe we developed a camaraderie that was maybe a little better than some other teams had.

"But the big difference was Doak. He could do things other people couldn't — and when we played with him, we could do things like that, too. He got most of the publicity, but because he was so totally unassuming, none of us ever resented it.

"In fact, when they did that *Life* cover in '48, we couldn't wait to see it — because we were all in it. When we got word it was out, I think about 50 guys rushed over to the newsstand to buy a copy.

"He made us all famous."

In their final act together, Walker could provide only inspiration, not help. But incredibly, the team that had played with him for three years played just as well as it ever had with him in the lineup.

Recalling the mighty effort against Notre Dame, however, Blakely has to laugh.

"The great sidelight to that game, of course, was little Johnny Champion blocking on big ol' Leon Hart," he says. "And it's true — Johnny did a magnificent job.

"Of course, he was lined up at wingback and what would happen was, Hart would charge into the backfield and Johnny would cut him down at the ankles with a slant block and Rote would run around him.

"Well, guess who the end was that Hart ran through all those times to get into our backfield?

"By the end of the day, I was a walking bruise. That guy nearly killed me — he was just unbelievable. That was the only game I played in four years at SMU where if we had had another game the next week, I couldn't have played."

But on that day, just like the rest of the Mustangs, Blakely stayed to the end. He was even the intended receiver on the pass Rote threw in a last desperate attempt to tie the score.

"We just messed that one up," Blakely says. "We even talked about it in the huddle — throwing to Champion in the flat. But something happened, and Rote tried to throw to me. The only problem was, there were about 18 guys between him and me — and one of them (Jerry Groom) intercepted it.

"At the end of the game, I was just too tired to worry about the outcome — we played our best and we lost.

"But afterward, I got a lot of satisfaction out of it — because nobody gave us a chance, and because, that whole game, I don't think the crowd ever sat down.

"I think there may have been a time that week when they were favored by 40 points, but it was at least four touchdowns at kickoff.

"But it wasn't a game like that. It was a game they will all remember."

A Mustang Who Needed a Bigger Stadium

The Cotton Bowl, circa 1947.

CHAPTER FOUR

On the first Saturday in October 1947, what had begun as a rather promising football career took its first sharp turn into the realm of legend.

On that evening, a crowd reported at 26,000 trooped into the Cotton Bowl — SMU's occasional lair at the time — to watch the Mustangs' home opener against Missouri. And early in the fourth quarter they saw something that, legend suggests, most of them never forgot. It was a 57-yard run by SMU's increasingly-heralded sophomore tailback, Doak Walker, that set the entire house agog.

A MUSTANG WHO NEEDED A BIGGER STADIUM

It was not a touchdown run — Walker was knocked out of bounds at the Missouri 20 — but it was a journey that left gaping witnesses in its wake and would still be discussed in reverent tones five decades into the future.

And in one sudden moment, it personified the era that was beginning for SMU: a flash of lightning, and suddenly a red-clad dervish was loose in the enemy camp, setting tents afire.

It swiftly turned the tide of battle and presented Mustang fans with a notion they soon grew comfortable with: whatever the need, whatever the obstacle, it would be Walker to the rescue.

It began as a simple sweep to the right — a play that Walker quickly deduced was going nowhere.

So he reversed his field, shedding Tigers here and there along the way, and was soon tearing up the left sideline.

When the pursuit hemmed him in at midfield, he suddenly veered right again and began to pick his way through some of the same black hats he had eluded earlier. Reaching the right sideline, he turned upfield until the pursuit finally ran him out of bounds.

At the conclusion of the run, 26,000 fans, 11 Tigers and most of Walker's own blockers were gassed, and SMU was threatening again.

Walker had already scored twice — once on a 76-yard punt return — and thrown a touchdown pass to build a 21-7 lead, but the Tigers had rallied for two scores to make it 21-19. It was there — after a Missouri kickoff put the ball at the SMU 23, that Walker pulled off his dazzling run.

SMU quickly scored — then recovered a fumble by the befuddled guests, and Gil Johnson threw a touchdown pass to Ed Green to wrap up a 35-19 victory. In addition to the punt return, Walker finished with 111 yards on 16 carries and completed four of seven passes for 54 yards.

It was his first appearance before the home fans in the all-America years of 1947, '48 and '49, and it was among the more memorable of his career.

It also showed off quite a bit of the Rusty Russell raz-

Doak and SMU waterboy, Timmy Trimble, posed for Life magazine during practice in 1948.

zle-dazzle to which Mustang fans would grow accustomed. The punt return came on a double-safety reverse that left forlorn Tigers skidding to a halt on the wrong side of the field.

And the touchdown following Walker's long run came on a Russell specialty — with Walker taking the snap, plunging straight ahead toward the middle, then handing off behind his back to Green, coming around on a wingback reverse.

The win boosted the Ponies to 2-0 on the season and put a considerable dent in the skeptical view that the freshman phenom of '45 would find the going tougher when the real men returned from the war.

When the season opened, it was felt that Texas — led by Bobby Layne — and defending co-champion Rice would be the cream of the league, with the Mustangs given a shot at being contenders due to their outstanding backs, including Walker, Dick McKissack and Paul Page.

At the time, Johnson was an unknown factor, although the situation changed rapidly.

As the Mustangs began drills for the opener against Santa Clara, the world heard from Dr. A. Powell Davies, who mounted the pulpit at Washington's All Souls Unitarian Church to denounce long skirts — the new fall fashion for women.

Describing the new fashions as "moronic, imbecilic and grotesque," the reverend called the new skirt lengths "immoral, because this will deprive the shivering people of Europe of the wool they need to keep them warm this winter."

In a somewhat different approach to the relief of war-ravaged Europe, the U.S. Government had launched the Marshall Plan, calling for massive shipments of food across the Atlantic.

With a spirit of national cooperation carrying over from the war, the administration even received a pledge from brewers and distillers vowing to use less grain for spirits, leaving more to be shipped overseas. In response, the Soviets began mustering support to combat this new wave of "American imperialism."

Elsewhere, a campaign was launched to create a wife for the cartoon character "Uncle Sam," since his 171 years of bachelorhood was not deemed representative of the

"Bulging with manpower and versatile skill, the visitors from Houston will have every advantage except for the brains and ability wrapped up in the person of the 175-pound sophomore tailback who grew up in the shadow of Ownby Stadium."

The Dallas Morning News

country's dedication to family values. It was decided that the bride would be named Martha and would be modeled after a composite of Jane Greer, Loretta Young and Linda Darnell.

And at Texas A&M, "rebellious" students who had been agitating for change off and on since the previous winter finally came to an agreement with the administration, in which all agreed to move forward together.

In San Francisco, the Mustangs beat Santa Clara, 22-6, with Walker scoring all three touchdowns — in progressively spectacular fashion.

After a short plunge for the first score, he reversed his field twice on a 44-yard run for the second. Then, after the Broncos scored in the fourth quarter, he ran the kickoff back 97 yards for the final SMU tally.

In each of the first two games, opponents received ample demonstration of Walker's startling change-of-pace — which along with his dauntless spirit was to become an enduring trademark. He left the San Francisco press raving about his broken-field talents, especially his ability to change directions effortlessly.

But it was after the Missouri game that the local skeptics began piling onto the bandwagon. Having had less than 24 hours to digest the news that Brooklyn's Cook-

ie Lavagetto had smashed Floyd Bevins' no-hit bid with two out in the ninth, they drifted quickly from the World Series to the amazing Mustang.

That week, one local columnist decided that Walker "has proven himself almost the equal of Layne as a passer; a great field general, team spark and clutch competitor; an outstanding climax runner, equally dangerous on kick returns, open-type plays, or power plays through the line.

"In the next three seasons, he could become the Southwest's first unanimous all-America backfield choice since the days of John Kimbrough and Davey O'Brien."

Next up was Oklahoma A&M, which fell, 21-14, as the Mustangs built up a three-TD cushion and then coasted. SMU wasted little time enhancing its reputation for trickery: the first touchdown involved two laterals followed by a pass from Walker to Sid Halliday.

But the sequence for which Walker is usually remembered came in the final moments, when he boomed a quick kick down to the A&M seven-yard line.

But Aggie return man Ben Aldridge scooped up the ball, turned upfield, picked up a convoy of blockers, and came rolling goalward on what eventually became a 79-yard return.

The fact that he didn't score was due to Walker — the last man between him and the goal. Patiently giving ground to the blockers, he finally saw his chance, darted through a gap, and nailed Aldridge at the 14-yard line.

Although the Aggies scored a meaningless touchdown with 30 seconds left, Walker was widely praised for his coolness in handling the blockers, an indication of the growing willingness to discover brilliance in his every move.

A&M was more impressed with him in another sense — at the end of the season, they placed him on their all-opponent sportsmanship team.

But while SMU was grabbing headlines, Layne and Texas were even more impressive — chewing up Choo-Choo Justice and North Carolina, 34-0, one week and Oklahoma, 34-14, the next, to break from the gate at 4-0.

A showdown between two old pals seemed to be brewing, but there were a few obstacles to be removed from the path first.

SMU had now opened a season 3-0 for the first time since the Rose Bowl year of 1935, but the Mustangs were underdogs in the SWC opener against defending champion Rice — which had lost a close decision to LSU, traveled to the coast to tie a Southern Cal team that eventually wound up in the Rose Bowl, and rolled over a pretty good Tulane team.

The game was billed as Walker against the Owls, typified by the following passage in The Dallas Morning News.

"Bulging with manpower and versatile skill, the visitors from Houston will have every advantage except for the brains and ability wrapped up in the person of the 175-pound sophomore tailback who grew up in the shadow of Ownby Stadium.

"Rice is said to be three- and four-deep in all positions and has speed, strength, spirit and savvy. SMU has Walker and the idea that he alone will make the contest even."

As matters developed, he made it a little more than that.

At the end of the day it was reported that he had scored once, carried 12 times for 87 yards, completed four of five passes for 33 yards, returned a punt 12 yards, intercepted two passes, and recovered a fumble.

When Matty Bell removed his star late in the third quarter, a forlorn Rice fan stood up and cheered, saying, "That looks like our best play of the day."

In a 14-0 game, Rice's best move was to the SMU 25-yard line in the first quarter. The Mustangs finished with 354 yards and rocked the visitors back on their heels throughout the day. For the third week in a row, Matty called off the dogs in the second half.

Through four games, Walker had scored 52 points, rolled up 469 total yards, averaged 31.6 yards on punt returns, was punting at a 51.3 clip, and was being hailed as the best all-around back in SMU history.

Following a logical progression, Bell proclaimed, "He was the best freshman the conference ever saw, and now he's the best sophomore. And I think next year, he'll be the greatest junior ..."

Around the league, the lowlight of the week was A&M's trip to Baton Rouge, which occurred in the midst of a Trailways bus strike. The team lost to LSU, and a busload of A&M fans was fired on as it made the return trip home.

Fortunately, no one was hit, and police concluded that the culprit was a disgruntled Trailways employee, who had failed to notice that the Aggie bus was a Greyhound.

The following week, SMU and UCLA seemed to be firing blanks — but once again, the Mustangs pulled of a spectacular play that led to victory.

It wound up 7-0, with the Mustangs using defense and an 86-yard pass play to survive the battle.

Both teams missed chances — UCLA twice fumbled inside the SMU five-yard line (Walker and Page recovering), and the Mustangs failed to score on four cracks from inside the three.

But midway through the fourth quarter, Johnson took a snap at his 12-yard line and hit Page on the sideline near midfield, and the fleet wingback was finally pulled down at the Bruin two-yard line. Walker scored on third down, and SMU won again.

With that victory, SMU acquired a Top-10 national ranking for the first time, and the stage was set for the great showdown — Rusty's boys, Layne and Walker, in a battle for supremacy in the SWC, and maybe more. One of them, of course, had the advantage that Rusty was still coaching him.

Doak and his SMU teammates at practice prior to the 1948 season.

With victories over Arkansas and Rice in addition to four non-conference triumphs, the Longhorns came in at 6-0 and were ranked third in the nation, behind Michigan and Notre Dame. The Mustangs were 5-0 and ranked eighth.

Befitting the occasion, SMU abandoned 23,000-seat Ownby Stadium for the Cotton Bowl (45,000), which was quickly sold out. Therein occurred the first inkling of what was soon to become a major concern: finding an arena large enough to hold the growing mass of Mustang fans. Over the next two years, the problem was solved by adding 30,000 seats to the Cotton Bowl.

There was the customary week-long buildup, centering on the duel between the two best friends — each about to try to ruin the other's season. Texas was still considered the stronger team overall, but by now nobody was taking anything for granted where Walker and the Mustangs were concerned.

On the day of the game, the great racehorse Man o' War died at the age of 30, having once set five world records and since becoming the leading money-winning sire of all time.

In Houston, the director of the local branch of the Museum of Natural History was attacked by a drunk coral snake.

Robert A. Vines explained that someone had brought the snake to the museum in a liquor bottle, which still had some liquid in the bottle. Assuming the snake was dead, he tried to remove it, and was attacked but not bitten. He killed the snake with a book.

In Dallas, the Longhorns were favored and the Mustangs were ready.

Texas kicked off, and Frank Payne dropped back into the SMU end zone to receive the booming kick. He ran a few yards upfield, then began drifting to the right, with the ball stuck on his hip, and the Longhorn pursuit drifted with him.

Suddenly, Page wheeled around behind him, going toward the left sideline, and the two executed the slickest handoff of the year.

A MUSTANG WHO NEEDED A BIGGER STADIUM

"I was standing right there, and I almost didn't see it because they did it so smooth," head linesman Harry Taylor would say later. "Page just whizzed past me and headed upfield, and I'll guarantee you that the Texas defenders over on the left side never knew he had the ball."

Billy Pyle finally cornered the streaking Mustang downfield, but the play worked for 81 yards and set SMU up at the Texas 19-yard line, as an overflow crowd of nearly 50,000 went limp.

The stunned Longhorns recovered quickly, holding the hosts to one yard in three plays. But on fourth down, Walker threw to McKissack, and SMU had a first down at the four.

Then, with the ball at the two, the Mustangs once again struck with their "flicker" play — Walker charging up the middle and then handing the ball behind him to Page, who swept left end for a 7-0 lead.

Thus was launched a see-saw struggle that lived up to every inch of its advance billing. Layne eventually passed for 120 yards, but the Longhorns had to contend all day with a collection of shifting, revolving defenses Bell had concocted for the occasion.

Scarcely outdone, Russell devised an offensive scheme designed to move Walker around so that Texas was never sure where he would line up or what he would do next. Before the day was over, he had played every position in the SMU backfield.

One post-game account described Russell's scheme as a "hooligan" offense in which "Walker and the wingbacks played here, there, and just about anywhere."

Early in the second quarter, Tom Landry dove over from the two at the end of a short drive set up by a punt return, and the score was tied, 7-7.

Shortly, SMU was on the march again, with Gil Johnson at tailback and Walker lined up at blocking back — from where he took a handoff and completed a crucial pass for a first down. Soon, however, he had drifted out to one of the wingback slots.

In light of Walker's later career, it is one of the stranger aspects of the 1947 season that through the first five games, he had not caught a pass.

By the time he left SMU — and certainly by the time

his career with Detroit was over — his ability as a receiver had come to be regarded as one of his more formidable skills. But for half a season, the Mustangs had not utilized it.

In part, this was because it had not been necessary. Of their five wins, four came relatively easy, and he was sufficiently useful as tailback, defensive back, kick returner and overall inspirational catalyst that they had simply forgotten to throw the ball at him.

Or maybe this was all part of some diabolical plot Russell hatched to pull on the Longhorns.

The more likely explanation is that he began the season as the tailback, and the idea of working Johnson in on passing downs grew gradually.

In any case, the first pass he caught that year may have been the most famous reception of his SMU career — partly because of a news photo that framed him leaping into the air for the ball while a frustrated Landry hurries over to try to stop it.

It was usually accompanied by some sort of caption indicating it as the play that beat the Longhorns.

"I've always gotten a kick out of that photo," Walker says, laughing, "because Tom was the defender."

Johnson threw it and Walker turned it into a 54-yard gain to the Texas two-yard line, from where SMU soon scored to take a 14-7 lead.

Layne brought Texas back 71 yards in the fourth quarter, but the Longhorns missed the extra-point attempt.

Then, they were back again, with one last chance. From the SMU 32, Jim Canady squirted through the line for 16 yards and an apparent first down, but Texas was offside.

Moments later, on fourth and two from the 33, Landry slammed into the line, but lost his footing and was stopped for no gain.

SMU took over and ran out the clock on a 14-13 game that hardly could have been closer. The Mustangs wound up with 199 total yards, the Longhorns 197.

"It was definitely one of those games," Taylor said, "where you really hated that somebody had to lose."

For the Longhorns, it was a bitter defeat. They finished 9-1, ranked fifth in the nation. SMU finished 9-0-1, ranked third.

From there, it was out of the pan and into the jinx for SMU — which departed for the Texas A&M game with full knowledge that they had not won in College Station since 1935. Come right down to it, they hadn't beaten the Aggies anywhere since 1938.

The streak indeed ended — though not in the expected fashion. Walker played with a leg injury — Matty had both legs taped so the Aggies couldn't tell which was hurt — and had a lackluster day. But this time it was Johnson and the defense that came to the rescue, as the Aggies fell, 13-0.

With Walker lining up at blocking back much of the game, Johnson completed 14 of 16 passes for 152 yards and both SMU scores. Page caught one of the TD passes and had an end zone interception to kill A&M's most promising threat. The defense held the Aggies to 13 yards on the ground and intercepted five passes.

Still, it was a tense game until Johnson drove the Mustangs 82 and 80 yards in the middle periods. After a 30-yard pass to Page made it 7-0 in the second quarter, SMU came out in a spread in the third quarter — with the wingbacks sitting eight yards outside the ends and Johnson hitting everyone in sight. Raleigh Blakely caught an 18-yard scoring pass in the third quarter and the contest was never again in question.

The following week at Ownby, questions were flying everywhere, along with a few other things.

The occasion was a visit from the Arkansas Razorbacks, who had been Cinderella co-champions the previous year but were having a sort of Ugly Sister year in 1947 and spoiling for an upset. Or a fight.

When the game was finally over, SMU had gained 306 yards, Arkansas 155, and the officials 126. The Mustangs won, 14-6.

During the afternoon, a total of nine penalties worth 81 yards were stepped off against the Porkers, who were not having a tidy game. The unfortunate nature of a couple of these, moreover, led to wounded feelings.

The first occurred on an SMU punt in the second quarter, when the Razorbacks were flagged for defensive holding. Halted at their 25, the Mustangs used the reprieve to complete an 81-yard march that wiped out a 6-0 lead Arkansas had constructed on a short first-quarter drive.

Doak checks the sports section of the Dallas newspaper to read about an upcoming opponent.

In the final period, a man identified as the Arkansas trainer shoved field judge Charley Hawn when he attempted to mark the spot where a receiver had stepped out of bounds in from of the Hog bench.

This occurred on a play in which Arkansas' Clyde Scott threw to Billy Bass, who rolled down the sideline until finally being tackled at the SMU 5-yard line. There, he fumbled the ball, and the Mustangs recovered.

Upfield, however, Hawn marked a spot where he said Bass stepped out, resulting in howls from the Arkansas bench and one brisk shove.

Spreading further cheer was umpire Rosco Minton, who arrived on the scene and called Arkansas for offensive shoving — pushing the Razorbacks back to their 30-yard line.

On the next play, they fumbled. SMU recovered at the 31 and drove in for the score that clinched the game.

At the end of the game, an Arkansas fan rushed from the stands and attacked referee Jack Sisco, who prompt-

A MUSTANG WHO NEEDED A BIGGER STADIUM

ly knocked his assailant down with a flurry of blows. He was attempting to press his counterattack when he was pulled off by the other officials.

The next week, the undefeated, nationally-ranked Mustangs rolled into Waco and were greeted by 12,000 fans — the usual number that can be mustered to sit and watch a game of Quagmire Ball.

Baylor's stadium had sat untarped through a week of heavy rains, and a Friday night football game had left it looking like a tributary of the lower Ganges. On a wet, frigid afternoon, the Mustangs and Bears sloshed through a scoreless tie that lasted 55 minutes.

For the game, Baylor managed four first downs and 72 total yards — all on the ground. The Mustangs had about twice that, plus a variety of turnovers, but they finally got a break on a short Baylor punt and found themselves looking at fourth and eight at the nine with five minutes left.

The situation clearly called for Walker to kick a field goal — something he hadn't done all year — so Johnson took the snap and placed the ball down on the 16. The ensuing kick was so low that the referee had to consult with the field judge before they agreed, in tandem, that it was good.

Page quickly intercepted a Baylor pass and SMU scored again, as the final score rose to 10-0 and the Mustangs rose to 9-0.

At this point, Walker & Co. had strung together five consecutive triumphs (UCLA, Texas, A&M, Arkansas, Baylor) in which the vanquished squadron departed the premises believing it could have won the game if "luck" had not embraced SMU at a critical moment.

In those days, "luck" was usually dressed in red and wearing No. 37, but the phenomenon had begun to draw considerable comment.

In one local column, it was noted that the Mustangs were now on the threshold of becoming the first SWC team to go through a season unbeaten and untied since the national championship teams at TCU in 1938 and A&M in '39 — but that this troupe did not carry the same "invincible" look of those storied outfits.

"These hair-breadth escapes," the writer began, "would indicate the SMU team falls short of the 'great' category. Yet it must have something, to continue getting by week after week.

"One of these 'somethings' is smartness.

"It may stem from sound coaching, the blessing of Methodism, or the cool noggin of young Doak Walker, the signal caller. Whatever it is, the Mustangs have yet to show any signs of disorganization, desperation or dissension.

"Always, in the eleventh hour, they remain poised — and confident of victory."

Nevertheless, on the eve of the TCU game, Fort Worth Star-Telegram columnist Lorin McMullen predicted that the lowly Horned Frogs would upset the nationally-ranked Mustangs.

These predictions had been floating around all year — but although McMullen's was based mainly on civic pride, it was the one that would turn out to be right.

Or half-right.

As the November 29 date with TCU approached, Walker learned that he had made at least one all-America team that year, even though none had been released yet. NBC sports director Bill Stern arrived in Fort Worth for the game on Friday and let it be known that when his prestigious team came out a week later, the SMU tailback would be on it.

"No way you could leave him off," he said.

Nobody announced anything about putting Lindy Berry, Pete Stout or Morris (Snake) Bailey on their all-America team, but Stern and the Mustangs saw a lot of them on Saturday.

The next day, 32,000 showed up in TCU Stadium for the annual renewal of the season-ending feud between those two lovable old chums, Dutch Meyer and Matty Bell.

Off the field, they were fishing buddies and kindred souls. On it they were bitter rivals who had long ago instituted a sociable custom for this game: whichever one drew the underdog card was honor-bound to concoct some nasty surprise to even the odds.

This time, as Matty prepared the SMU defense to counter the TCU spread, Meyer brought the Horned Frogs out in a single wing right with Charles Jackson flanked left, tightened the blocking lanes, and began running the fullback (Stout) inside. Meanwhile, the sophomore passing combo — Berry and Bailey — began attacking the secondary.

The Frogs came in at 4-4-1, their main achievement having been a shocking 20-7 win over Oklahoma in Nor-

55

man — but three of their losses had been by a touchdown and they had tied a team (Kansas) that was going to the Orange Bowl.

In fact, they had already accepted a bid to the Delta Bowl in Memphis, where they would face Mississippi.

For their Cotton Bowl foe, the Mustangs had chosen unbeaten Eastern champion Penn State — a memorable decision, since it brought to Dallas the first two black players (Wally Triplett and Dennie Hoggard) ever to play in that bowl.

But this was hardly on their minds in Fort Worth, especially after the Frogs drove 50 yards for a touchdown in the early moments. Berry hit Bailey with a pass that carried to the 13, then rammed Stout through the Ponies four times for the TD.

But this was to be a day on which even the purple-draped TCU fans would grudgingly admit that Doak Walker was one incredible football player. By the end of the day he would accumulate 475 total yards, wearing out every player on the field — including himself.

He served notice of this after TCU's touchdown by returning the ensuing kickoff 77 yards, but the Mustangs were unable to score.

Early in the second quarter, Orein Browning intercepted a pass and returned it 56 yards to the SMU 12, and TCU quickly scored again.

With his team down, 12-0, Walker retaliated quickly. Skirting a TCU rush, he swept around the Frog flank and turned an aborted pass play into a 61-yard scoring

Doak played in the outfield for the SMU baseball team in 1947-1949.

run. Then in the third period he scored at the end of a 51-yard drive to put SMU ahead, 13-12.

It stayed that way until there were two minutes left in the game, with the Frogs sitting at their 20. Then Berry hit Bailey with a 20-yard pass, and the lanky end began zigzagging downfield, eluding Ponies as he went. He was finally tackled at the 15, but before going down he flipped the ball backward to Jackson, who kept running until the

A MUSTANG WHO NEEDED A BIGGER STADIUM

Mustangs finally brought him down at the eight.

On the next play, Berry began an off-tackle smash, but when he was stopped at the five he pitched out to Stout, who had swung wide and sailed untouched into the end zone. With 1:40 left, TCU led, 19-13.

The following sequence has been enshrined in legend as perhaps the one play in Walker's career typifying his collective abilities — not least of which being poise under pressure.

Taking the kickoff at his six-yard line, he began a meandering journey that carried him back and forth up the field, patiently waiting for blockers and setting TCU tacklers up like so many bowling pins. As he passed the SMU bench, he yelled at Bell, "Get the old man ready!"

Startled, Bell signaled for Johnson, who was dispatched into the game when the Frogs finally cornered Walker at the TCU 36 after a 58-yard return.

On third down, Johnson hit Walker, who made a leaping catch downfield, and with 20 seconds left, SMU was at the 10-yard line. On the next play, Johnson hit Sid Halliday in the end zone, and the score was tied.

And while admirers and pundits have spent 50 years praising the runback, the presence of mind, the coolness in the face of disaster, Walker's clearest memory is of the play that followed the touchdown.

"I missed the damned extra point kick!" he says, seeming as disgusted with himself today as he was then. "By the time we got down there and scored, I was pooped, and I should have called time out to rest.

"Instead, I just lined up and kicked it, and cost us a chance to win the game. That's the main thing I remember about that day."

At midfield, Dutch and Matty shook hands and congratulated each other, old chums again.

In addition to the historic presence of Triplett and Hoggard, the game played on January 1, 1948, was also the first Cotton Bowl game pitting two undefeated teams against each other — with SMU ranked third coming in and Penn State — led by Fran Rogel — ranked fourth.

It was also Walker's 21st birthday, which he celebrated by scoring once, throwing a touchdown pass, and accumulating 125 total yards against what was considered the best defense in the country.

But after SMU gained an early lead, Elwood Petchel brought the Nittany Lions back, and the two teams battled to a 13-13 tie.

The Mustangs drove 82 yards on their first possession, climaxed by a 53-yard pass from Walker to Page. They scored again late in the half — Walker going over from the two — but the conversion attempt was blocked.

But with 14 seconds left in the half, Petchel threw a 38-yard touchdown pass to Larry Cooney, a third-team reserve who had played only 10 minutes during the season, and the tide began to turn.

In the third quarter, Petchel threw a scoring pass to Triplett, but Ed Czekaj missed the extra point, and it stayed 13-13. On the game's final play, Hoggard dove for a Petchel pass in the end zone but couldn't hold it.

When the Nittany Lions returned to the Cotton Bowl 24 years later, Czekaj — then the AD — walked out on the field before the game and tried the extra point kick again. He made it, but the one that counted had sailed wide years earlier.

"I really think we should have won that game," says Walker, who finished with 125 total yards, "but after we got the lead we started playing cautiously. That was something we normally didn't do, but for some reason we played a strange game that day."

In Memphis, TCU carried a lead into the fourth quarter against Ole Miss before Charley Conerly guided the Rebs to a pair of TD's and a 13-9 win. Mississippi (9-2) was actually the Southeastern Conference champion, although Alabama and Georgia Tech — playing in the Sugar and Orange bowls — were the league's highest-ranked teams.

In New Orleans, Bobby Layne threw for 183 yards in his last collegiate game as the fifth-ranked Longhorns rolled over the sixth-ranked Crimson Tide, 27-7.

So, in games where they did not face each other, the two pals from Highland Park finished the season unbeaten, and Walker won the Maxwell Trophy.

He had led the SWC in rushing (740 yards) and scoring (94 points) and led the nation in kickoff returns (10 for 38.7). He had passed for 411 yards while catching eight passes and intercepting five.

Raised to Be an All-American

It was a bright summer afternoon, and a group of Dallas schoolchildren were happily splashing and playing in a large neighborhood swimming pool.

The boys were particularly daring — darting in and out between the floats, showing off their swimming skills. And suddenly, disaster struck.

One of the boys got his bathing suit hooked on a peg below the water line, and couldn't work himself free. He was trapped underwater, floundering, losing air, panicking ...

And then, his friend came and saved him.

"Even then," Dick Davis says, "Doak Walker was a hero.

"He saved my life. If he hadn't come down there and gotten me off that hook and pulled me to the surface, I would have drowned ... right there in that pool, 6 years old."

Surviving to proceed through a happy childhood, a football career at SMU, and 46 years at Merrill Lynch (he retired this summer), Davis says he has never known anyone quite like the pal who fished him out of the pool that day, long ago.

"We grew up together, starting off as next door neighbors over in East Dallas," Davis says. "Then both our parents moved into that Highland Park neighborhood, and starting in kindergarten we lived three blocks apart.

"We used to spend the night at each other's house, and

All-America halfback Charley (Choo-Choo) Justice of North Carolina visits with Doak prior to the 1950 Cotton Bowl.

in later years we used to double-date together. He was the most unassuming guy you could ever meet — and all through his life, he never changed.

"But if you wanted to be an athlete, you had to compare yourself to Doak."

Frank Payne knows the feeling.

In 1946, Payne — a freshman from Breckenridge following in his father's footsteps — was the SMU tailback. He was elevated to the post abruptly during the third game of the season.

"In the first two games, we'd lost one and tied one," he says, "and then we played Oklahoma A&M and we

"Wherever we were, he was the most popular guy in school. And the main reason was, he was truly an outstanding person, but he never acted like it. There was no conceit, no arrogance. He would be the last person in the world to act like a big shot — and that came from the home. Doak's father literally raised him to be an all-American. I don't mean an all-American football player. I mean an all-American boy."

Dick Davis

were trailing at the half.

"It didn't make me much difference, because I was about 21st on the depth chart, so while Matty (Bell) was making his half-time speech, I was just sittin' there drinking a Coke.

"Then as he starts back out the door, he looks at me and says, 'Payne, you'll start at tailback this half.'

"It happened so fast I never had time to get nervous, and I had the best game of my career. I completed 12 of 14 passes — two for touchdowns — and we won the game."

From there, the Mustangs proceeded to a 4-5-1 finish (4-4 with Payne at tailback), but at least managed to create a little momentum with lopsided wins over Baylor and TCU at the end.

"Then, going into the '47 season," Payne says, "there was all this publicity about Doak coming back. That's all anyone was talking about, and the tailback job had pretty much been conceded before practice started, according to the papers.

"I had heard of him, but that's about all. I figured, he can't be that good, and I determined that I was going to give him a real battle for the job — because I figured it was still mine."

He is now Dr. Frank Payne, a leading pediatrician in Dallas, where he has raised a family and maintained a practice at the same office location for 37 years. Recalling the three years he spent as Walker's backup, he laughs.

"Well," he says, "with Doak and then Kyle (Rote) around, I sure wasn't going to get much playing time.

"But ... that was such a wonderful time. I don't regret a minute of it."

A common feeling, it seems ...

"That whole era ... those were the happiest times of

Doak always attracted a large crowd whenever he appeared in public in his hometown of Dallas.

my life," Davis says, "and Doak was around the whole time — grade school, Highland Park, and then SMU.

"Wherever we were, he was the most popular guy in school. And the main reason was, he was truly an outstanding person, but he never acted like it. There was no conceit, no arrogance. He would be the last person in the world to act like a big shot — and that came from the home.

"Doak's father literally raised him to be an all-American. I don't mean an all-American football player. I mean an all-American boy.

"They were happy times, and they were times that developed tremendous personal loyalties. Growing up, he was more a brother to me than my brother was."

But, Davis says, Walker also had a fiercely competitive nature, especially about athletic contests.

"I think that may have been the source of the great friendship between him and Bobby Layne when we were at Highland Park," he says. "But it was of a slightly different nature.

"With Bobby, it was all up front — he'd bite your arm off to win. It was maybe more subtle with Doak, but just as intense. If you beat him pitching horseshoes, he'd go off and practice for weeks and then come back and invite you to a rematch.

"I remember that game when we were juniors when we lost to San Angelo by one point in the playoffs and that ended our season. We had 'em beat, but they came back.

"The next year, Bobby had graduated, but when we got to San Angelo in the playoffs again, Doak remembered. He had a terrific game and we won, 39-6.

"The only problem was, we lost the next week in the finals."

Davis says that despite the cloak-and-dagger aspects of the famous trip to New Orleans and the ride back in '45, there was little doubt where Walker would wind up going to college.

"Growing up, we all had heroes," he says. "Mine were Joe Medwick and Stan Musial. Doak's was Harry Shuford.

"Besides, the relationship between him and Rusty was like a father-son thing."

While Russell may have looked upon Walker as a son, he regarded the rest of the Mustangs as apprentice wizards.

"We all had a lot of fun playing for Rusty," says Payne. "He was very innovative, and it was fun just seeing what he would come up with next. He picked up things nobody else would have thought of.

"I remember a game where Doak started rolling to the right on a pass play, but nothing was open, so he ran back to the left and wound up with a gain on the play. A little while later, I did the exact same thing myself.

"The next week, Rusty put it in the offense."

Payne's personal favorite was the famed opening kick-off maneuver against Texas in 1947, when he and Page befuddled the Longhorns with a full-speed exchange that resulting in an 81-yard runback, setting up a touchdown.

But while Rusty taught the Mustangs to try the unexpected, his star pupil turned the tactic into an art form.

"Doak was a very talented player in a physical sense," Payne says. "But the thing that made him great was the way he thought on the field.

"I guess the one moment I'll never forget was that first sequence in the Texas game in '48. It was a big revenge game for them, and they were really laying for us. I think they had burned Doak in effigy, or something.

"When we got to the stadium, it was jammed [68,000], and those people were yelling so loud you couldn't hear the signals. The first two plays after the opening kickoff, they crushed us. The team and the fans

> "The reason he was such a great player was that he did everything well — he had a lot of different ways to beat you. But also, he was a smart player and an inspirational leader."
>
> *Frank Payne*

were about as pumped up as you could get.

"Then on third down, Doak dropped back, and they were all around him, but he kept slipping out of tackles and running around, and pretty soon he starts drifting to the sideline, and then he was running toward the goal line and he had them scattered out all over the field.

"He ran about 67 yards for a touchdown, and all of a sudden you could have heard a pin drop in that stadium. One play, and he just took that crowd out, cool as you could imagine, and we ended up winning easily (21-6).

"But, he was always doing stuff like that."

Life with Russell and Matty Bell, Payne says, was almost like joining the circus.

"They coached us hard and worked us hard," he says, "but they also believed in making sure we had fun. Each year, we would take a long train trip to either the East Coast or the West Coast — great trips. We played tough intersectional opponents, but when the game was over, we relaxed well.

"When I was a freshman, we went up to Philadelphia and played Temple. But instead of heading home after the game, Matty put us on a train for New York, and we went to Radio City and watched a show.

"On the way back from Pittsburgh one year, we stopped in St. Louis and went to a Cardinals baseball game. When we went out to Santa Clara we were gone probably a week, sightseeing.

"And after our second Cotton Bowl game, the coaches said we deserved a trip because we had played two bowls in our own stadium. So during mid-term break, the whole team went to Mexico."

Throughout all this, Payne says, Walker remained a dazzling player on the field and a quietly modest teammate off it.

"How would I describe him?" Payne says, with a shrug. "All American.

"The reason he was such a great player was that he did everything well — he had a lot of different ways to beat you. But also, he was a smart player and an inspirational leader.

"Otherwise, he was a normal guy and never conceited. I remember one night we took our girlfriends to a movie, and there was a newsreel about Doak winning the Heisman Trophy. And when they showed him making his acceptance speech in that high-pitched voice of his, he just sat there and laughed at himself."

In 1949, Payne figures, "I guess we got paid back for all those last-minute wins we piled up the two previous years."

And when Walker was felled by the flu at midseason, Payne started at tailback for the first time in three years. His moment in the sun, however, was brief.

"About the middle of the second quarter," he says, "I made a terrible mistake — I tried to block one of those big Kentucky ends."

He repaired to the sideline with a mangled finger. The team doctor examined it briefly, yanked it once, and taped it to the adjacent digit.

"I went back into the game," he says. "They didn't find out until later that the thing was broken."

But although their final season was proving less rewarding on the field, the spirit of those who had ridden through two glittering campaigns with Walker never wavered.

"By the end of the year, we had so many people hurt — even I was starting," Davis says, laughing. "But we had been a pretty mature bunch of guys when it all started — and we had had so much fun playing together, that our spirits weren't really dampened much. We realized our problems were mainly due to injuries, and there's not much you can do about that.

"Sometimes, I look at players these days, and I wonder if they really enjoy it as much as we did."

It was, Davis says, "a golden era in the Southwest Conference." It was due, in part, to Matty Bell, who he likens to Winston Churchill and St. Paul.

"He was one of the fairest, most point-blank men I ever met," Davis says, "and a most interesting person. Matty could cry anytime he wanted to."

Payne has a similar recollection.

"They used to call him 'Moanin' Matty,' " he says, "because every week he cried about how bad off we were. But he took care of us pretty well.

"When I was ready to graduate, a guy from Rockwall showed up to talk to me. They were looking for a coach over there, and the job sounded pretty good to me, since I didn't have one at the time.

"But Matty put an end to that pretty quickly. He got rid of the guy, and then he called me in and said, 'Look, I've got plenty of guys on this team who can be coaches. I've only got one who is going to be a doctor. You're going to medical school.'

"But you know, I'm really proud of the guys I went to school with at SMU. You'll have a few in every crowd who'll have a drinking problem or something — but as far as being cheats or crooks, we don't have any.

"We all seem to have turned out pretty well, and I love 'em all because they're just good folks."

They were also an exceptional team, although, Davis says, "Doak was really the difference between us and everybody else."

But in their final act, without him, they achieved perhaps their finest moment. The spirit that carried them to a near-upset of Notre Dame, however, was by then a familiar one.

Doak rips past the Texas defense in 1948. He scored two touchdowns in the Mustangs' 21-6 win.

"We were so banged up that we had a lot of guys in the lineup that really hadn't played much," Payne says. "But by that time, we had gotten so used to the idea that we could play with anyone, we didn't worry about it. I don't remember us ever being afraid of anyone.

"I also think we had a good chance to at least tie that game, because on an early drive, I think Kyle Rote scored but the officials didn't give it to him.

"I think he broke the plane, and by today's rules it would have been a touchdown. But back then, you had to actually wind up in the end zone, and he got pushed back."

But for Davis, who played both ways in the middle of the line, the game is memorable enough as it stands.

"That was as good a football game as you could possibly ask for," he says, "because of how good they were and how well we played. We were prepared, we never gave up, and I don't know if we could have played any better.

"They were favored by four touchdowns, but we were loose going in. I had to play center on offense, and the first time we lined up I looked over there and there was

that big all-American tackle, Jim Martin. He had a tattoo on his arm that was bigger than my leg.

"So I bent over the ball and I asked him, 'You ever play against a spread before?'

"He shook his head, so I said, 'Well you'd better move over some.' And he did.

"We had a tip on the way their center held the ball, up or down, pass or run, so we knew what they were doing on each play — we just didn't know where it was going. We just played them a helluva game."

When Notre Dame's Billy Barrett scored the winning touchdown late in the fourth quarter, he had to drag his back leg over the goal line — with Davis firmly clamped to it.

"He drug me over the goal line," Davis says, smiling. "I was trying to pull him down, but I just couldn't do it."

Reflecting on the last day of the "Doak Walker Era", Davis smiles again.

"That Notre Dame game ... was truly what SMU football was all about at that time.

"We had lived in a golden era, and it was a good way to end your career."

COLLIER'S 1948 ALL-AMERICA

| Quarterback | DOAK WALKER | S. M. U. |

CHAPTER SIX

A Heisman Season to Remember

In September 1948, two of the most prominent individuals in America — each lavishly splashed with almost continuous publicity — were proud native sons of The Great State of Texas.

One was an SMU football player named Doak Walker. Although his first name was actually Ewell, by now most people seemed to think it was "Undefeated."

The other was a New Deal politician and rising figure in the Democratic Party who, through recent adventures, had acquired the nickname "Landslide Lyndon."

Each day, it seemed, one or the other — frequently both — would be prominently displayed in the newspaper. And if the average reader had been questioned on the possibility that either of these gentlemen would one day be president of the United States, the reply would have been immediate and forthright:

"Why, yeah ... the guy in the red helmet looks like a good bet."

Normally, Walker resided on the sports pages. On Page One, in news accounts of the day, the president of the United States could usually be found fighting Communism. And over in the next column, Lyndon Johnson and Republican incumbent Coke Stevenson could be found fighting an equally nasty battle for a U.S. Senate seat.

September was not one of The Great State's finer months, but it was certainly eventful.

For Johnson and Stevenson, the battle for a spot on the November ballot became, in political terms, a life-or-death struggle, and was waged viciously. When a mysterious late surge by Johnson wiped out a Stevenson lead, the future president innocently reminded everyone that the same thing had happened to him in 1941, with the opposite result.

At one point, with nearly a million votes cast, Johnson appeared to be the winner by 17 votes. Later, the margin increased to 287, and LBJ gave an address to "my fellow citizens" assuring them that he had won "by a comfortable margin."

But Stevenson supporters were soon digging up evidence of murky activities in remote South Texas counties such as Jim Wells, Zapata and Duval, which brought in late returns overwhelmingly in Johnson's favor.

Included in these was a margin of 4,622 to 40 from a largely rural county reputedly run by a political boss known as "The Duke of Duval" that was considered a highway for the entry of illegal immigrants.

There were heated suggestions that many of those Johnson voters actually resided in local cemeteries, or had recently resided in another country. There were reports of ballot boxes disappearing, records being lost, voters vanishing. At one point, Stevenson won a temporary injunction, and there was talk of a federal investigation.

Finally, on September 28, a federal district judge overturned the injunction, and declared Johnson the winner. He won the senate seat in November, and a famous political career was solidified. Stevenson, the West Texas rancher, gradually disappeared from the political scene.

By that time, there were people in the Catskills who had heard of the Duke of Duval, and the state was nursing a collective black eye.

Then, in keeping with the normal scenario of the day,

a dashingly handsome Mustang came riding to the rescue.

When the September 27 issue of *Life* magazine hit the newsstands, Doak Walker was on the cover. In that era, it was tantamount to having a statue of oneself placed in every town square in America.

And at that point, an amazing transformation occurred. The Mustang star ceased to be simply an all-American football player and became ... Doak Walker, all-American.

Handsome, polite, painfully modest and armed with the brilliance to escape sure disaster on a weekly basis, he was instantly adopted by fans from Cape Cod to San Luis Obispo as the model hero of the post-war era. By the time he left SMU, he had appeared on the cover of 47 magazines.

In 1947, the Mustangs had been an entertaining team with an amazing knack for victory. In '48, personalized by the spread inside the magazine, they became the toast of America.

They were clean-cut, daring, prone to "Thank You" and "Yes, ma'am," and inclined to point out a coach or teammate when asked about the key to success.

Instead of pulverizing hapless foes like some of the resident national juggernauts, they won with style and poise against foes that were their equals in terms of size and strength. Win or lose, they were invariably gracious when discussing the opposition.

And thanks to Rusty Russell, they had an offense from Mars.

It was to be another brilliant season, one that began with a high-profile romp in Pittsburgh and ended with a frustrated Dutch Meyer — foiled again at the last moment — stomping on his hat in the Cotton Bowl.

For a topper, the Mustangs this time were victorious in the Cotton Bowl game, and Walker won the Heisman Trophy.

They arrived for the season opener in Pittsburgh riding a huge pre-season buildup centered around Walker, prompting a local columnist to declare, "Evidently, we are about to be visited by the most outlandish Texan since Pecos Bill."

Perhaps the Panthers could have handled Pecos Bill, but they were woefully unprepared for Russell's acrobatic

The 1948 Mustangs posted a record of 9-1-1, including a 21-13 win over Oregon in the Cotton Bowl.

aggregation — which now included a dazzling sophomore and future all-American named Kyle Rote.

The hosts were bigger and stronger, but the Mustangs were faster, smarter, and armed with a passing game that produced 241 yards and four touchdowns. Overall, SMU generated more than 400 yards on offense and rolled to an easy 33-14 win over a Pittsburgh team that would finish 6-3, losing only to Ohio State and national champion Notre Dame the rest of the way.

Even now, the Panthers' befuddlement brings a chuckle from Walker.

"To most people," he says, "Rusty's offense looked like a bunch of people milling around in a bus station. But I had spent so much time over at his house in high school, learning all the variations, that I finally reached a point where I knew what he was thinking at a given time. I felt very comfortable with it.

"The main thing about it was, we just had a lot of fun doing it, and that was due to Rusty. But you definitely knew the aerial circus had arrived when we hit town.

"The Southwest Conference was incredibly strong in

those days, and the teams that saw us on a regular basis did a little better dealing with our offense. But it was really a lot of fun when we went on the road to play one of those Eastern teams that had never seen it."

Indeed. With the Panthers keying on Walker, Russell kept shifting him around and inserting Johnson in the tailback slot — from where he threw nine passes and completed all of them for 207 yards and three touchdowns. Admirably democratic, he threw one TD pass to Walker, one to Rote and one to Raleigh Blakely.

In a development common to the Mustang offense at the time, Walker threw one touchdown pass and caught another. And, just so the Panthers wouldn't think all that publicity was overdone, he zigzagged through the whole crowd on a 76-yard punt return for the other SMU score.

"One of the keys to our success back then was that we all played so well together," Walker says. "In that era, of course, most of us were still playing both ways, and we got a lot of expert coaching from both Matty and Rusty.

"Matty probably didn't know three plays in the offense — but he had been one of the best defensive

"The main thing about it was, we just had a lot of fun doing it, and that was due to Rusty. But you definitely knew the aerial circus had arrived when we hit town."

Doak Walker

coaches in the country for 20 years. We never went into a game with just one defense — we'd have a half-dozen. He was as innovative that way as Rusty was on offense. We were running a 4-3 and a 4-4 some of the time, and back then, nobody had ever seen that.

"But one of the biggest reasons why all that worked is that we were a smart team. Maybe by today's standards we weren't big or fast or super-talented, but we were all smart, and eager to learn. We got along well together and we did a lot of things together. And every time the coaches wanted to try something new on us, they had the right bunch for it.

"Rusty used to carry a briefcase around, and I think it had about three or four hundred plays in it. When we played teams that were unfamiliar with us, it was very hard for them to adjust. When we played teams in our own league, he always had something special cooked up for that game to give us an edge if we needed it."

The biggest edge, of course, was a tailback who could turn an off-tackle smash into a newsreel highlight, and there is much truth to the notion that every offense is as

good as its personnel. But Russell had been beating people with this offense for 20 years, and he never had personnel that fit it better.

It was based on the single wing, the dominant offense of the century's first 50 years. It featured a tailback set deep at the back of the formation, with a fullback in front of him and slightly to the right or left (the I-formation is a single wing with a quarterback) and a blocking back near the line, usually in front of the fullback. The wingback was set out on the flank, outside the end.

Russell regularly twisted this into a double wing, with two flankers, or a spread, with only the tailback deep. The Mustangs also used a "Y" formation with the tailback and fullback side-by-side, and moved the blocking back up and down the line.

It as an offense of sufficient flexibility that in a particular game, all four backs might carry the ball, or catch it, or throw it.

By 1948, one of the great advantages to the offense was that Walker and Rote could be moved at will to any point in the formation. Paul Page was normally the wingback, Dick McKissack the fullback, and Johnson — when he was in the game — was a tailback. But Rote and Walker rotated regularly between tailback and wingback, with Rote also lining up at fullback and Walker at blocking back.

End Sid Halliday, a co-captain and mainstay of the '47 team, had graduated, but Blakely and Bob Folsom were skilled receivers, and the Mustangs had a formidable lead blocker stationed on either side of the line — 200-pound tackle Joe Ethridge on one side and co-captain Frank (Brownie) Lewis on the other.

It was an offense based on deception, with spins, laterals, reverses, hidden ball tricks and flea-flickers.

It was the end of the great era of the "triple-threat tailback," who could run, throw or put the foe in a hole with a sudden quick kick. Fullbacks were famed for the spin-buck, which sent them hurtling into the line to keep the defense massed at the center, vulnerable to the sweep.

Russell's version added endless variety. Fullbacks smashed up the middle, threw the ball, or went deep on pass routes. Blocking backs spun like dervishes, hiding a quick snap and faking to one back while giving to another on a counter or reverse, or sometimes threw or received a short pass. Wingbacks were all over the field.

Often, when SMU snapped the ball, it seemed as if a giant red pinwheel had been set in motion.

In the second week of the 1948 season, this pinwheel struck Texas Tech's unfortunate Red Raiders flush on the jaw.

Then in the early stages of an ultimately successful lobbying campaign to gain admittance to the SWC, Tech had opened the season with two consecutive wins — including a 20-14 victory over Texas A&M a week before the SMU game.

But the SMU defense intercepted two passes and held the Raiders to 33 yards in the air, and the offense did the rest, as the Mustangs rolled to a 41-6 victory.

It was a truly cooperative venture, as Walker carried only six times for 59 yards and a touchdown, and completed two passes, one for a score. Matty called off the horses in the third quarter and the subs completed the rout.

It boosted the Ponies to a No. 4 national ranking behind Notre Dame, North Carolina and Northwestern, but was ultimately significant as a historical footnote.

The Mustangs' feverish following had now grown to such proportions that 23,000-seat Ownby Stadium, the on-campus facility, was no longer adequate as a home arena for the nation's most exciting team.

For their next home game, three weeks later against Santa Clara, the Mustangs moved permanently downtown into the Cotton Bowl, which had an official capacity 46,200 but could handle enough overflow to seat 50,000.

By the end of the year, that would also fall a little short of demand, and by the time Oregon arrived for the Cotton Bowl game, an upper deck had been added, increasing the capacity to 67,431.

It became known as "The House That Doak Built."

In the midst of the growing euphoria, however, a 15-game unbeaten streak that Doak had helped build was severed by Missouri, 20-14.

On the same day, in the Mustangs' new home in Dallas, Oklahoma defeated Texas by the same score, snapping an eight-year losing streak against the Longhorns.

The SWC was not a festive place that week.

The national "Hero of the Week" was Cleveland southpaw Gene Bearden, a knuckleball pitcher who was equipped with a metal plate in his head and another in his leg due to having his ship split in half by a Japanese torpedo during the war.

Improbably, he returned to win 20 for the Indians in 1948, and in the week between SMU's games with Tech and Missouri, he cut down the powerful Boston Red Sox in the American League's first-ever playoff, then came back on Friday to shut out the Braves in the World Series.

The game in Columbia — before a then-record Mizzou crowd of 30,892 — was hardly a shutout, but it wasn't much fun for the Mustangs.

Walker intercepted a pass, scored at the end of a first-half drive, and later caught a 74-yard scoring pass from Johnson, but it wasn't enough. The Tigers completed only one pass for 11 yards, but they ran through the SMU defense for 356 yards and won the game with more ease than the final score suggested.

Part of the reason why Missouri ran so easily through SMU was the absence of the Mustang guards — Brownie Lewis, who missed the game with an injury, and Walter Robards, who left the game with an injured arm that was soon adorned with a cast.

Neither was able to suit up for the conference opener against Rice, and with both Page and Rote nursing shoulder injuries, the Ponies were a sad lot when they departed for Houston.

As usual in those days, the Owls were a highly regarded bunch, but when Rice halfback Sonny Wyatt came streaking out of the chute with the opening kickoff, he was a man in trouble.

The Mustangs unhinged him at the 32, the ball popped into the air, SMU recovered, and as a then-record throng of 32,000 (before Rice Stadium was enlarged) stared in silent wonder, a 33-7 rout commenced.

After the fumble, Walker directed a short scoring march, which he capped himself from the two, in typical fashion. Bouncing off a wall of defenders on his first thrust, he charged back in a slightly different angle and scored.

Then Johnson took over, completing seven of 10 passes for 130 yards — three of them for touchdowns. The first went to Walker and covered 42 yards, with the shifty all-American using his broken field skills to cover the last 30 steps. On the next drive, Johnson flipped a shovel pass to Rote — who was not playing like a man with one healthy shoulder — for 20 yards to the Rice 10, then threw to McKissack for the score.

He threw to McKissack again — 22 yards — for a third-quarter score, and the reserves mopped up, with Frank Payne throwing to Gene (Chicken) Roberts for a final tally.

The Mustangs were obviously back in their old form, and had a national statistical leader to prove it — Johnson. In four games, he had completed 33 passes in 44 attempts for 574 yards and seven touchdowns. His total playing time had been 48 minutes.

As the Mustangs prepared for their first home game as permanent tenants of the Cotton Bowl, there were rumblings of a war to the death between the National Football League and the All-America Conference, which had been created after World War II and consisted of the Cleveland Browns and a large cast of extras.

"Any conciliation between the leagues now is impossible," said Philadelphia Eagles owner Alex Thompson, who had been acting as peacemaker for two years. "I've made my efforts, and now the hell with it."

In Dallas, Matty Bell figured he had his own problems. Arriving in the Cotton Bowl that week was Santa Clara — the storied West Coast school that was nearing the end of its days as a major football power and was gearing up for its last great flash of brilliance before extinction — a Sugar Bowl triumph that would come a year later.

Coached by Len Casanova, the Broncos were 4-1 with victories over Oklahoma (which began a 31-game winning streak the following week) and Stanford. Their only loss had been to unbeaten, Rose Bowl-bound California, and they had scored at least three touchdowns in each of their games.

"I don't know what we're gonna do," said Bell. "I mean it this time. I'll settle for a one-point win."

If this was intended to be a set-up, it worked beautifully — although the ensuing 33-0 romp was probably due to the fact that SMU was on a roll.

Walker threw a 20-yard touchdown pass to Rote at the end of a 77-yard drive in the first quarter, then he and Page bamboozled the Broncos with a fake reverse punt return out of a double safety.

Page kept the ball and rolled 65 yards before being knocked out of bounds at the Bronco 15 by the elegantly named Saxon Wraith, and Walker subsequently threw an 11-yard scoring pass to Blakely.

Rote ran through Wraith on a nine-yard trip at the end of an 82-yard drive in the third quarter, and Moanin' Matty sent in the reserves.

In the fourth quarter, Bill Weatherford threw 52 yards to Zohn Milam to set up a score by Chicken Roberts, and Payne threw a TD pass to Johnny Champion.

The Mustangs rolled up 434 yards while the Broncos — who would have to wait until '49 for their last moment of glory — managed six first downs.

Although he was pulled in the third quarter, Walker managed 98 yards on 10 carries in addition to the two perfectly thrown TD passes, prompting one of the writers traveling with the Broncos to declare, "If Walker isn't an all-American then neither was Chief Red Cloud."

Meanwhile, "The Great Ambush" was being prepared in Austin, where a local paper derisively referred to the Mustangs as "the darlings of the national magazines and pictorials" and Longhorn fans had worked themselves into an unusual frenzy.

In 1947, there had been little doubt that Michigan and Notre Dame were the two most powerful teams in the nation. But SMU had captured the No. 3 ranking by virtue of an unbeaten season highlighted by that 14-13 win over Texas — which had subsequently finished 10-1 with lopsided wins over North Carolina, Oklahoma and Alabama.

It had been one of the Longhorns' greatest teams ever, its glory partially eclipsed by those same Mustangs who were now doing more magazine layouts than Clark Gable.

Revenge was much on the collective mind in Austin, where fans were burning candles, building bonfires, holding midnight pep rallies, and pretty much behaving like Aggies.

Beaten by North Carolina and Oklahoma, the Longhorns seemed less formidable without Layne — but they were still the team SMU would have to beat to repeat as the conference champion.

They had also won 16 consecutive games at home, and were exceedingly peeved that the Mustangs were favored to win. No visitor to Memorial Stadium had come in as a favorite since Texas A&M in 1940, and on that occasion the Aggies had seen a 20-game winning streak snapped.

As for the stadium itself, 2,500 seats were hastily added, boosting the capacity to 68,750, and Texas officials estimated they could have sold 20,000 more tickets had the seats been available. On game day, it was the largest crowd in SWC history.

And in a matter of moments, Walker reduced it to tears.

When the Mustangs came up to the line for the third snap of the game, they were facing third and seven, a raging Texas defense and an immense, braying mob in the stands.

Taking the snap, Walker began looking for a receiver, as three Texas defenders bore down on him. Evading the rush, he began drifting slowly to his right, still looking downfield. Gradually, he picked up speed, then suddenly swept around the Texas end and was rolling down the sideline, with Page in front of him.

At the Texas 45, Page cut down Billy Pyle, the last defender, and Walker was gone, 67 yards. So was the crowd, and ultimately the game.

In a frustrating afternoon, Texas eventually rolled up 393 yards, but scored only once, cutting the SMU lead to 7-6 in the second quarter.

SMU, with 284 total yards, answered with two key fumble recoveries and the customary Mustang verve. They never trailed, and the menacing Texas crowd never got back into the game.

In the second quarter, Joe Ethridge plucked a Longhorn fumble out of the air and placed the Mustangs at the Texas 34. Johnson moved it to the three with a trio of strikes to Blakely, and Walker scored from the one.

In the third quarter, a fumble recovery by Robards and an exchange of punts set the Mustangs up at their 41, from where they rolled downfield on Johnson's passes. At the 18, Walker threw a five-yard pass to Blakely,

who tipped it to Rote trailing behind him, and SMU had a 21-6 lead that stood to the final gun.

In the aftermath, a bewildered observer wrote that, except for the 67-yard run, Walker hadn't done much, "except for scoring two touchdowns, starting the third drive with a pass, completing two passes, catching three passes, punting for a 46-yard average, selecting the plays flawlessly, blocking well and playing all four backfield positions. Mainly — it was just that in 55 minutes of double-duty service — he never made a mistake."

The Longhorns made several, and the road to the championship was now wide open. Soon, it began to narrow.

It was an oddity of the 1948 season that, having easily disposed of the two main title contenders, the Mustangs began to have extreme difficulty with the rest of the field.

After the Texas game, SMU stood 5-1 and had outscored its collective foes by a 175-53 margin. Over the final month of the season, the Mustangs faced a pugnacious quartet that finished 6-15-3 in SWC play and outscored them, 54-39, winning three and tying one.

But SMU wasn't the only prominent institution losing steam that week. Five days after the Mustangs beat Texas, The Chicago Tribune elected Thomas Dewey president of the United States, somewhat prematurely.

Later that day, newly re-elected president Harry S. Truman stood grinning widely and holding aloft the edition of "The World's Greatest Newspaper" with the banner headline, "Dewey Defeats Truman."

At that, the Trib was lucky no one handed Truman a copy of the earliest edition, which proclaimed, "Dewey Wins By Landslide!"

Two days later, the Cotton Bowl was graced by the presence of 53,000 fans and the Texas Aggies — who, not having won a game all year, tossed caution into the upper deck and lined up in an SMU-style double wing.

It almost worked. The only problem was that the key ingredient was still on the SMU side of the ball.

Matty Bell had a record of 79-40-8 at SMU and led the Mustangs to four Southwest Conference titles in 12 seasons, including a berth in the 1936 Rose Bowl.

Things opened badly for the Aggies when future governor Preston Smith fumbled the opening kickoff and Page recovered for SMU at the A&M 26. Walker threw to McKissack for the touchdown moments later, and the day began pretty much as expected.

In the second quarter the Aggies had a stiff wind at their backs but it seemed of rather little use when Walker broke off a 40-yard touchdown run to make it 14-0. Operating out of the "Y" formation, he faked a handoff, spun through the middle of the line, veered left and outraced Bob Goode down the sideline to the end zone.

It looked like another long line of march for the Cadets, but at this point they brought Buryl Baty in to run the double wing and he started floating balls downfield with the breeze.

It paid off just before halftime, when he hit Goode for 48 yards to the SMU seven. Switching back to the T, the Aggies scored on a pass off a double reverse three seconds from intermission.

Taking the wind in the third quarter, A&M drove to another score, and suddenly the top and bottom of the league were dead even.

Not for long. Walker took the ensuing kickoff, turned upfield, slanted toward the sideline, and raced past Page — at which point the two Mustangs executed a fake handoff.

With half of the Aggies chasing Page, Walker got past everyone but Goode — who tackled him at the A&M 38 after a 57-yard return.

SMU reached the 27 with a first down, and Walker then tossed 15 yards to Blakely at the 12.

On the next play, the Aggie pursuit followed him as he drifted to the right looking for a receiver. None emerged, so he suddenly cut back across the field in the opposite direction and trotted over the goal line.

Another valiant underdog effort foiled by Dastardly Doak.

The next week, SMU dropped into Fayetteville, where they were graciously welcomed by an overflow crowd (23,000) and a band of Razorbacks that had been simmering for a year.

In the esteemed view of the locals, a hefty injustice had taken place on the previous meeting at Ownby, and it

was time to set things square. What transpired was among the most heart-stopping of SMU's numerous "miracle" escapes of the period.

It was, among other things, a day on which two all-American backs were carried from the field on the same play. In the end, it was a day on which the Razorbacks — for all their certainty that they had been over-flagged a year earlier at Ownby — fared worse on their own field.

It was originally figured as a duel of all-Americans — Walker against the Razorbacks' Clyde Scott — but as the first quarter closed, both were on the bench, one of them for good.

Scott ran the opening kickoff back 50 yards, and Arkansas moved in quickly for a 6-0 lead. But with 30 seconds left in the quarter, the big Razorback star went down with torn knee ligaments and never returned.

On the same play, Walker went out after being rolled up by the Razorbacks' down-field blocking, but he returned six minutes deep in the second quarter. Midway through the third quarter, Leon Campbell outran Walker and Folsom on a 68-yard scoring journey to give Arkansas a 12-0 lead.

SMU finally retaliated when Rote scored on a short run after a 75-yard drive, and Walker kicked the extra point to make it 12-7. But in a flash, the Razorbacks were sitting at the Mustang 3, threatening to put it away.

A game-saving tackle by Blakely ended the threat, and finally, late in the game, SMU began riding Johnson's passes toward an astounding finish. At any point along the march, one play could have changed destiny for the Razorbacks, but they never got it.

When SMU seemed stopped at the Hogs' 36, Walker sent McKissack storming through a defense spread for the pass and he got 11 yards and new life. Then from the 20, Johnson was intercepted, and it seemed the Miracle Mustangs were dead. But Arkansas was called for being offside, and SMU had the ball at the 15.

Johnson then lofted a looping pass that Zohn Milam caught as he fell backward out of the end zone, but he was ruled out of bounds.

There remained two seconds on the clock when Johnson drifted back and fired a dart at the flag. Page caught it and fell into the end zone at the feet of defender Billy Bass, who had been the subject of the furor the previous year. SMU won, 14-12, and the Razorbacks — flagged 14 times for 121 yards, were seething.

"We kinda bunched up and stuck close together leaving the place," Johnson says, "because the crowd was all around us and they were plenty upset. We played that team twice while I was at SMU, and both times it was a little scary leaving the field after the game."

There was also unrest in the Big Ten — where an Iowa City attorney had dashed off an indignant letter to University of Minnesota president J.L. Morrill concerning the conduct of famed coach Bernie Bierman during a sporting engagement with the Hawkeyes.

The attorney/fan, Jack C. White, professed to be appalled at Bierman's profanity-laced retorts to some "kidding remarks" by Iowa fans sitting behind the Minnesota bench. Bierman also reportedly told Iowa coach Dr. Eddie Anderson that he would "never again bring a team here to play in front of this noxious crowd."

Bierman, who had coached the Golden Gophers to three national titles, later addressed reporters in Minneapolis, saying he had not seen White's letter but wished to assure everyone that it contained "numerous fallacies and inaccuracies."

Some may have thought it fallacious and inaccurate that Baylor had a chance to win a Cotton Bowl berth by beating SMU (in the Cotton Bowl) that week — but the recently lowly Bears played the Mustangs near dead-even for 60 minutes. After viewing the contest, however, one local scribe decided that it was "sort of an optical illusion."

His point was that although the final score was only 13-6, and the Methodists had led by a mere point until there were 45 seconds left, this was due mainly to the fact that they seemed content to just play well enough to win.

There was a certain logic involved, since the Ponies held a 280-106 edge in total yards and Baylor's only significant offensive thrust was a 28-yard scoring drive set up by a 25-yard punt return.

That one snapped the Mustangs out of their lethargy, and Rote ran 25 yards for a TD on the flicker play, with Walker's extra-point kick providing a 7-6 lead. Finally, the hosts wore down the thinner Bears on a late TD drive.

Rote actually dragged two exhausted Bears for part of a 20-yard run, which set up his 19-yard scoring sweep on the next play. He was the offensive star for SMU with 118 yards on 20 carries.

The victory left SMU at 5-0 in SWC play and assured of its second straight trip to the Cotton Bowl. Texas (4-1) could still share the title if TCU beat the Ponies, but SMU was the league representative on the strength of the win over the Longhorns.

Also that week, SMU announced the initiation of a series with Notre Dame, with the first game scheduled for 1949 in Dallas.

On Thanksgiving Day, Texas A&M's winless Aggies enacted one of the strangest conclusions to a season ever witnessed by tying Texas, 14-14, erasing any hope of a title tie for the Longhorns.

The following Saturday, in the nation's annual "Game

> We played (the Razorbacks) twice while I was at SMU, and both times it was a little scary leaving the field after the game."
>
> *Gil Johnson*

of the Year," winless Navy met undefeated Army, and the game ended 21-21.

In the first week of December, invincible Notre Dame met frequently invincible Southern Cal, and was deadlocked, 14-14.

And on the day the Midshipmen foiled Army's plans, 67,000 sat in the newly bedecked Cotton Bowl and watched lowly TCU tie the Mustangs. Again.

This time the score was 7-7. There were fewer offensive fireworks, but possibly even more drama.

Once again, the Horned Frogs — coming in at 4-5, were considered no reasonable match for the Mustangs (8-1), who now had the home-field advantage and one of the largest crowds in history on their side.

Once again, Dutch Meyer had planned something weird.

The offensive concoction was similar to that of the previous year — based on spreading the Mustang defense out and then slamming it inside — except this time the Frogs carried it to something of an extreme. Noted for being as aerially-prone as the Ponies, TCU completed one pass (of six attempts) for 14 yards.

But with blocking schemes designed to trap the SMU guards and leave the linebackers vulnerable, Pete Stout (15 carries for 119 yards) and Lindy Berry (21 carries for 117 yards) led a ground attack that churned out 308 yards.

Similarly, a wide-tackle six with a frill here and a flourish there limited the potent SMU runners to 68 yards on the ground. This left it all up to Gil Johnson — invariably referred to in game accounts as "the balding war veteran" — who was more than equal to the task.

In the second quarter, Berry slashed through his right tackle for 13 yards and a 7-0 TCU lead that lasted ... almost forever.

Berry and Stout brought the Frogs downfield again, but when they reached the SMU 6, they had time left for only one play before the half. After a delay penalty, they missed a field-goal attempt from the 19.

As the teams struggled through a scoreless second half, that seven-point lead seemed to grow, like a balloon slowly being pumped full of air.

And when TCU's Leon Joslin dropped a punt out of bounds inside the five, and an offside penalty subse-

> "At that time, I really had never heard of (the Heisman Trophy). And I certainly couldn't spell it. But I figured it must be some kind of big deal, because Matty was all excited about it."
>
> *Doak Walker*

quently pushed SMU back to the one-yard line, the balloon seemed to fill the whole stadium.

The clock showed 1:48 remaining, and SMU was 99 yards in the hole.

In came Johnson, with his thinning hair, his banged-up knee, and a nerve sufficient to burst TCU's balloon.

Standing in his end zone, he began firing a spread of passes at the Frogs, one of which connected with Zohn Milam for breathing room at the 27.

Then, the unthinkable happened: the center snapped the ball, and Johnson lit out at a gallop. By the time the Frogs chased him down, he and his gimpy knee had made it to the SMU 41 — and out of bounds to stop the clock.

After an incompletion by Champion, Johnson dropped back and fired 24 yards downfield to McKissack, who went out of bounds at the TCU 35.

Now, there were 15 seconds left. Johnson took the snap

A popular target for defenders, Doak often had to change his game jersey.

and handed off to Walker, who began to swing wide to his left. But as the pursuit swung toward the SMU all-American, it became suddenly evident that the handoff had been a fake.

Johnson drifted right, then straightened up and threw to Milam — the only individual in the entire stadium who was standing in the end zone.

He caught the ball as time expired, and Walker kicked the extra point that saved the Mustangs. While 67,000 exploded in varying emotions, Meyer stood on the sideline, staring at the field.

Slowly, he removed his gray felt hat, raised it high

above his head, and slammed it to the ground. He gazed at it for just a moment. Then he stomped it.

A few moments later, Meyer and his battered fedora met Bell and his crinkled grin at midfield.

"Hello, snakebit," Bell said. "Really had us beat. Just amazing ..."

"Yeah," Meyer said. "You're right."

In the TCU locker room, Meyer found an obscure corner and stood, leaning against the wall, drinking a soda, speaking to no one.

On a nearby bench, a huge tackle sat staring at the floor, muttering over and over, "ninety-nine yards in a minute and a half; ninety-nine yards in ..."

Max Eubank hugged Billy Moorman and said he thought TCU should have won.

"But you've gotta hand it to those Mustangs," he said. "They sure can pull 'em out of the fire."

And assessing back-to-back ties the following day in The Fort Worth Star-Telegram, Irving Farmer wrote, "The Methodists and the Christians are still tied, without benefit of clergy."

When the Mustangs had whipped Baylor to clinch the Cotton Bowl berth, Bell had polled his players on their choice of New Year's Day opponent (as was the custom in those days), and came up with a list featuring North Carolina at the top, followed by Georgia, Oklahoma, Tulane and Clemson — all of whom had put together glittering seasons.

But by the day of the TCU game, with North Carolina leaning toward a Sugar Bowl date with Oklahoma, the choice for the Cotton Bowl had shifted to Oregon.

Although the Ducks had lost only to Michigan and were co-champions of the Pacific Coast Conference, they had been counted out of the bowl picture because the PCC's annual policy was to send one team to the Rose Bowl, period.

That team was the other co-champion — unbeaten and higher-ranked California, which had not played the Ducks during the season.

But when some Oregon students successfully lobbied the Orange Bowl for a bid, the PCC granted the school special permission to play a post-season game. Their destination turned out to be Dallas.

Their leading scorer was a feisty halfback named John McKay, but the key to Oregon's success lay in a towering, rifle-armed quarterback destined to become famed in the NFL as "The Flying Dutchman" — Norm Van Brocklin.

In early December, the SWC faculty committee wound up its winter meeting with a secret ballot rejecting applications for membership from Texas Tech, Hardin-Simmons and Houston.

Tech, with 6,500 students and an 18,500-seat stadium, would finally gain admittance eight years later, and begin league play in football in 1960. Hardin-Simmons would

never make it, and Houston would finally be admitted in 1976.

By the time of the vote, Walker and Russell were in New York for a dinner at the Downtown Athletic Club, where Walker was honored as the 1948 winner of the Heisman Trophy.

"At that time, I really had never heard of it," Walker says. "And I certainly couldn't spell it.

"But I figured it must be some kind of big deal, because Matty was all excited about it."

Accompanying Walker to New York were his parents, his sister, Pat, his girlfriend, Norma Peterson, and Russell.

"I always thought it was a nice touch that Matty chose Rusty to go up there with me," Walker says. "Usually, your head coach goes with you — but I think Matty sent Rusty because it was his offense we were running."

On December 21, the war between the NFL and the All-America Conference ceased long enough for the two to hold a joint draft. The last-place Chicago Rockets of the AAC chose Nevada's Stan Heath, who had broken Davey O'Brien's NCAA total offense record.

Detroit, the last-place team in the NFL, chose Georgia quarterback John Rauch — then, through a pre-arranged deal, quickly traded him to Boston of the AAC for the future rights to Walker.

And so, because Boston had wanted to swipe Rauch away from the rival New York Yankees, Walker's NFL future was set on a fortunate course.

Two days later, seven convicted Japanese war criminals — including former premier Hideki Tojo — climbed the 13 steps to the gallows in Tokyo's Sugamo Prison.

In a final letter to his wife, the man who had led the Japanese war effort had enclosed a poem: "The cold moon ... many eras has it lighted ... and is now here."

After being hanged, the seven were cremated, and their ashes scattered in the wind.

On New Year's Day, most local papers led with a photo of Walker and Rote, running side-by-side, each carrying a football.

For the Ducks, it was to be a prophetic vision.

The game turned into probably the best tandem performance the two all-Americans ever produced: Walker scored once, gained 66 yards on 14 carries,

THE HEISMAN

In 1948, Doak rushed for 598 yards and passed for 383 yards.

if on cue, when it reached the goal-line flag. Rote's traveled 84 yards, to the Oregon 12.

The Mustangs launched an opening scoring drive in each half, and thoroughly dominated the game whenever they chose to. When Oregon finally cut the SMU lead to 14-6 with a fourth-quarter score, the Ponies answered with another touchdown drive.

Van Brocklin played well in defeat (145 passing yards and a touchdown) and with a late drive the Ducks closed the score to 21-13 and created a 387-337 edge in total yards, but coach Jim Aiken wasn't fooled.

"They are definitely the better team," he said, "and the difference was Doak Walker. He can pass, he can run, and he can kick. He was particularly effective because we were afraid of what he could do. We had to loosen up our defense because Walker was so good."

It was Walker's 22nd birthday celebration, played to an audience of 69,000, plus the TV crowd. The Cotton Bowl enjoyed its biggest gate in history ($309,526.60), and each team took home a record $108,912.47.

It was, overall, a big day for the SWC, as Baylor topped Wake Forest in the Dixie Bowl and Tom Landry led Texas to a shocking 41-28 rout of SEC champ Georgia in the Orange Bowl.

completed six passes for 79 yards, caught a seven-yard pass and called a brilliant game. Rote ran 16 times for 93 yards, caught four passes for 55, and had a 36-yard scoring run.

And as a national viewing audience on the fledgling medium of television sat, enthralled, each pulled off a prodigious quick kick in the second quarter, when SMU had a stiff wind at its back.

Walker's traveled 79 yards and rolled out of bounds, as

For the regular season, Walker had rushed for 598 yards, passed for 383, caught 16 passes for 285, averaged 16.9 on 10 punt returns and 32.2 on five kickoff returns, returned three interceptions 75 yards, punted for a 44.0 average, and led the SWC in scoring with 96 points.

He was again a consensus all-American and had added the Heisman to his list of trophies.

Along with the hearts and minds of thousands of hero-worshipers.

A Pair of Mustangs Who Passed the SWC Dizzy

It was autumn, 1946, and Gil Johnson — World War II veteran and recent arrival at SMU — was addressing the assembled members of the press.

As Johnson proceeded with an account of his existence up to that moment, a nearby scribbler suddenly stopped and stared at him, amazed.

"Hold it!" he said. "Did you just say you have a roommate named Frances?!?"

Gazing coolly at his interrogator, Johnson drew him closer and said, conspiratorially, "Why yes, didn't they tell you?

"All of us guys who just came back from the war ... they issued each of us a woman."

This answer was about half jotted down before it dawned on one and all that ol' Gil was a tongue-in-cheek sort of guy.

But it was a persona that fit Johnson, a balding combat veteran with a gimp knee, almost perfectly.

For in the wide and varied offense of Rusty Russell — "Mr. Russell," as Johnson calls him to this day — there was always room for a man with a special skill and a dramatic presence.

And for two years, in 1947 and '48, that man was Johnson — a specialist who couldn't run much on a bad leg,

but threw well enough to be drafted after his junior year.

It became a familiar scenario through those two magical seasons: just when the opposing defense thought it had that dratted Doak Walker corralled, in would come Johnson, with a smirk on his face and six points up his sleeve.

Frequently, the man on the receiving end of the crucial pass would be Walker — whose ability to move around in the formation enhanced Johnson's effectiveness.

Used with increasing regularity, Johnson was the Southwest Conference passing leader in 1948 and ranked sixth in the nation, with 78 completions in 128 attempts for 1,026 yards and nine touchdowns.

More significant than numbers, however, was the impact Johnson often had on opposing teams. He was often used either to provide an overwhelming opening shock — as in 1948 at Pittsburgh — or to come in at a crucial moment late in the game and deliver the saving blow.

As for that 1946 roommate ...

The individual in question was actually Francis Pulattie — a fellow war veteran and fierce blocking back who was generally regarded as being anything but cuddly.

At the time, the two were living in a tent at Ownby Stadium.

"There were about 15 of us out there," Johnson says. "We had all come back from the war, and Matty (Bell)

PASSING THE SWC DIZZY

wasn't quite sure what to do with us. We were all there on kind of a make-good trial basis. We slept out there in the stadium and took our meals in the girls' dorm."

Coming out of Tyler a few years earlier, Johnson had briefly gone to Texas A&M, but soon left because, "I was pretty sure I didn't like the Army."

He wound up in the Navy instead, and spent three and a half years on a submarine in the Pacific.

"It was an experience," he says. "We operated a lot around Midway and Johnston Island, but when the war ended we were in the Kuril Islands, north of Japan. From there, we went all the way back to New York to muster out, and it was a long trip.

"We had some scrapes, but I survived. We got three destroyers after us once when we sank a couple of transports carrying Japanese troops.

"Our maximum depth was about 300 to 360 feet, so we had to sit down there while they dropped 186 depth charges on us, but we finally got out of it.

"It's a feeling, I can guarantee you, like no other. You sit down there and wait, and sweat. The sweat runs down your body and finally it fills up your boots.

"I was on the Swordfish once, but they took me off, and right after that it was torpedoed and sunk."

Like many returning veterans, Johnson had few precise post-war plans, "except that I knew I wanted to

go to a co-ed college."

So he enrolled at SMU as a physical education major, with a vague plan to follow the footsteps of his brother — Bill (Tiger) Johnson, who wound up playing pro ball with the San Francisco 49ers.

"Funny deal," he says, "a few years later, when I was playing with the New York Yankees, I dropped back to pass against the 49ers, and one of those big ol' linemen got hold of me and was fixin' to kill me.

"And all of a sudden another guy yelled at him and said, 'Hold it — that's Tiger's brother!'

"So the guy who had hold of me stopped and just laid me down on the ground real easy.

"After he quit playing, my brother stayed up there in the NFL, as an assistant or a scout, and he's been doing it ever since.

"In other words, he's never actually

"Overall, Doak was the most publicized athlete that I ever remember. But the way he handled it, there was never a moment's resentment."

Gil Johnson

had a real job in his life.

"But it's a good deal. Not long ago, I asked him what it is, exactly, that he's doing now, and the answer was kinda vague.

"So I just haven't asked about it since."

Returning as golden conquerors, the vets were, of course, given a hero's welcome and enjoyed lavish treatment wherever they went.

"Matty," Johnson says, "was very suspicious of us. He kept reminding us to behave ourselves, because we were around a bunch of kids fresh out of high school.

"He told us these kids were very impressionable and we had to watch what we did around them. He said, 'If you have to smoke a cigarette, go outside behind a tree — and don't let me catch you walking around campus with a can of beer.'

"We went to some kind of orientation speech, and one of the big administrators got up and welcomed us all to SMU.

"Then he told all the freshmen girls to stay away from the veterans.

"I remember he told them, 'I promise you, we will put a floodlight in every bush on campus if we have to.'

"It kinda made you feel right at home."

Johnson soon had other worries. Claiming prior jurisdiction, A&M coach Homer Norton moved to have him declared ineligible for the 1946 season.

"Right before we opened against Temple, they did it," Johnson says. "The league had a meeting and voted on it, and I lost, 4-3.

"So, here I damn near got killed in the war, and I come home and they're saying veterans will be given the benefit of every doubt, and I work my tail off to make the team, and a coach at A&M gets me fired."

Welcome home, ya big lug.

After SMU's so-so season in 1946, the vets reported for spring drills in '47, and irritation stepped up a notch.

"Everybody kept talking about some guy named Doak Walker coming back, and how great he was, and that's all you heard," Johnson says. "We were still pretty fresh out of the war, and we weren't too interested in any talk about any 'hero.'

"But after a few days, everyone's attitude began to change. Doak had an effect on people like that. I know that at his first camp in Detroit, some of the veterans really tried to cut him up at first. But he made fools of 'em.

"With us, after a few days it was obvious what a tremendous athlete he was."

But the key aspect, Johnson says, was the attitude.

"Overall," he says, "Doak was the most publicized athlete that I ever remember. But the way he handled it, there was never a moment's resentment.

"You could tell that because, if there is, it will always show up in practice. Some guy starts gettin' too big, some of those big ol' linemen will do something about it in practice.

"But it never happened with us. We got behind him and started winning, and he made heroes of us all.

"His father had put him on that track. Mr. Walker was

a great educator, and he sort of molded a great many young people over a period of time. He did that with his son, and he did a great job."

There was also "Mr. Russell's offense" — which was so simple, Johnson says, that a kid could run it. Or an "Old Man."

"Mr. Russell was a genius," Johnson says. "He used to carry this notebook around with 200 to 300 plays in it, and he could always come up with something new for each game.

"It was a wide-open, pass-oriented offense that appealed to the fans and was guaranteed — if you ran it right — to pick a defense to pieces. It was easy to win with that offense.

"But the other big factor was Doak. He was the key to the offense, but he was also so versatile that he could move anywhere — wingback, blocking back — and wherever he moved, the defense shifted. Whatever he did, the defense followed it, and you could use him as a decoy and be free to do anything else you wanted."

This was never more evident than in the fading seconds of a nerve-jangling battle that provided Johnson with a couple of his favorite memories at SMU — the 7-7 tie with TCU in front of 67,000 in the Cotton Bowl, in which the Ponies whisked 99 yards quicker than you could say, "Mr. Russell is a genius."

"One of the reasons that game always brings back memories is because I got to run the ball on a crucial play," Johnson says. "I just remember the play being wide open — because they [Horned Frogs] were so surprised."

The second reason is the play — "Fade 66 Right" — on which Johnson faked a handoff to Walker moving left, drifted to the right, and threw 35 yards to a wide-open Zohn Milam in the end zone as time expired. The Frogs were so sure that Walker had the ball that they neglected to cover the passer, or the receiver in the end zone.

"The third reason," Johnson says, grinning, "is the memory of Dutch Meyer stomping on his $100 Stetson."

It was Johnson's second last-minute rescue in the final three weeks of the season — the other being the pass to Paul Page that beat Arkansas, 14-12, on the game's final play.

"That one was really strange," he says. "After the game, hundreds of fans came down out of the stands and surrounded us. I thought they were going to start something, but they just kind of milled around, looking at us, like we

were from outer space or something."

Although the forces of reason had decreed that SMU women should stay away from veterans, Johnson had an ace in the hole — he needed tutoring.

That's how he met Shirley, a coed the university paid $2 an hour to help Johnson with his studies. Soon, Bell noticed them taking in a movie together, and later asked Johnson if something more than tutoring was in progress.

"Yeah," Johnson said. "You're paying for that, too."

They have now been married 48 years, raised four children, and have lived in the same house near White Rock Lake for 42 years.

In the spring of 1949, Johnson signed a contract with the New York Yankees that ended his SMU career prematurely.

"I kind of hated to leave," he says, "because they had signed that contract with Notre Dame for the 1949 game, and I was kind of looking forward to playing in it.

"But we had just gotten married, and when the man came down from New York and laid $5,000 down on the table, I just couldn't resist it. I played one season.

"The years I spent at SMU were really wonderful years. I made a lot of friends, and developed some good business contacts in the community that have lasted throughout my life.

"Eventually, I went to work for Humble Oil. I started running a service station, and by 1968, I was making so much money I had a heart attack."

Now retired and living comfortably in the house by the lake, Gil and Shirley retain a few mementos from the SMU days, such as the photo on the wall taken from a spread in *Collier's* magazine.

And, oh yes, the immense wall photo in the garage.

It is a blowup of a photo taken 49 years ago. Gil and Shirley found it a few years ago, weather-beaten, discarded in an alley behind an establishment where it had hung for years. They carted it home and spruced it up.

Stretched across the front of the frame are four Mustangs running in a line — the backfield with which SMU opened the 1948 season. The names roll off the lips of longtime SMU fans like a chronicle of immortals ... Johnson, Walker, McKissack, Page ...

"We really played well together," Johnson says, "and we had an awful lot of fun doing it."

Collier's

15c

December 10, 1

The 60th All-America

CHAPTER EIGHT

America's Favorite Cover Boy

In early November 1949, the editorial board of *Collier's* maga-zine received an unusual letter from a college football player. The editors at that time were busily preparing their annu-al college football issue, which included an all-America team selected by coaches around the country.

It was the era of the great weekly magazines in America, and *Collier's* was one of the most popular and influential. Its all-America team ranked with those put out by the wire services, and was an extreme-ly prestigious event, accompanied by articles and color photograph spreads.

When the editors received the letter, they were shocked. The young football player had learned that he was being considered for a place on the team, and had decided to write a letter in a blatant attempt to influ-ence the selection process.

It read, in part:

"I deeply appreciate the fact that the coaches are considering me for the all-America football team, even though illness and injuries have kept me out of the lineup so much this season. However, I believe there are other all-America candidates who have seen more action and therefore are more deserving of consideration. Being selected on the coaches' team last year gave me one of the biggest thrills I've ever had in football. I know the players who are named to this year's all-America (squad) will be just as appreciative of the honor."

It was signed by Doak Walker.

He sat down and wrote it one day, then put it into an envelope and dropped it in a mailbox on his way to class, without mentioning it to anyone. He never told his coaches, his teammates, or his family.

The first anyone knew of it was when *Collier's* editor Bill Fay sent a copy of the letter to SMU publicist Lester Jordan.

It was a simple, straightforward gesture ... but it probably did more to define who Doak Walker was than all the dazzling runs, the stirring victories, the forest of trophies, or the millions of words written about him.

In response, the magazine honored his request — picking an all-America backfield that included Arnold Galiffa of Army, Charley (Choo-Choo) Justice of North Carolina, Lynn Chandnois of Michigan State and Emil Sitko of Notre Dame.

This was accompanied, however, by a cover photo of Walker and his fiancee, Norma Peterson, and a special award inside that ran with the all-star team. The magazine reprinted his remarkable letter and named him "The Player of the Year for Sportsmanship."

The same day, The Associated Press simply took the conventional approach and named him to its all-America team for the third consecutive year.

But in truth, it had not been a banner year for the Mustangs — who after two seasons of miraculously dodging every bullet fired at them, finished the season limping and shot full of holes.

Then, in one final magnificent gesture without their fabled leader, they cast themselves in bronze ... forever.

In the news of the day as September arrived, there was continued street fighting in Berlin, the U.S. government sent Marshall Tito $20 million so he could fight Commu-

nism, and a 15-year-old girl in Coeur D'Alene, Idaho, killed her father with a hammer when he failed to take her on a trip, as promised.

And in Stephens County, four hunters were startled when a 40-pound block of ice fell from the sky and landed a few yards from them.

"It was kind of milky-white," one of them told authorities, "and it tasted like soap."

As for SWC football, it had definitely hit a peak. Inside the league, no one was safe; and most of them could beat just about anybody outside the league. The Cotton Bowl had been expanded — again — to satisfy the community's growing need to watch Walker perform Saturday afternoon miracles.

"Never in all my experience have I seen so many teams so nearly equal," said TCU's Dutch Meyer, assessing the upcoming season. "It should be the greatest race we've ever had."

A case in point was Texas A&M, which came in with a bevy of sophomore backs including Dick Gardemal, Bob Smith, Glenn Lippman, Billy Tidwell and Yale Lary — and finished last.

At the other end of the spectrum was Rice — which had future All-Pro Tobin Rote at quarterback, all-American James (Froggie) Williams at one end, all-American Joe Watson at center, future all-American Bill Howton trying to break into the lineup, and a collection of running backs so deep that when starter Van Ballard broke his collarbone, he was simply replaced by super-soph Billy Burkhalter.

After rolling through the league — with hair-raising escapes against Texas and TCU — the Owls (10-1) chewed up North Carolina in the Cotton Bowl and finished the season ranked fifth in the nation.

Baylor (8-2) was a surprise second-place team, but the Bears were no fluke: Adrian Burk (1,428 yards) was the nation's leading passer, and receiver J.D. Ison was a second-team all-America.

Texas outscored its foes, 290-93, ranking in the Top 10 in both scoring and total defense, but somehow managed to lose four games by a total margin of 10 points. The Longhorns were led by Paul Campbell, Randall Clay, Ben Procter and all-American guard Bud McFadin.

TCU's versatile Lindy Berry ranked third in the nation

in total offense and sixth in punt returns, and the Frogs were the fifth-best passing team in the country, but split six conference games, going 6-3-1 overall.

Twice during the season the Frogs overcame a three-touchdown deficit to avert defeat (once with a tie), and nearly did it a third time against Rice. In five games at TCU Stadium, the Frogs and their guests totaled 34 TD's.

As for SMU, one pre-season analysis began thusly: "If it were not that the incomparable Doak Walker is back for his farewell tour, one would be tempted to herald a sudden decline of Southern Methodist University football."

This was a little steep, but the Mustangs, despite an early report that they were "frisky," did indeed have problems, although the Cotton Bowl had been enlarged — again, to 75,000 — to accommodate the crowds.

Page, the incomparable wingback, had graduated, and Johnson had gotten married and signed a pro contract. Brownie Lewis, Joe Etheridge, John Hamberger and David Moon were prominent among several absentees among linemen and linebackers.

But this did not make SMU a dead pony. In addition to Walker, Rote, McKissack, Frank Payne and Johnny Champion, there was sophomore Fred Benners, who would throw for 3,370 yards in the next three seasons. Raleigh Blakely, Zohn Milam and Bobby Folsom made up an able receiver corps.

It was still a potent team, but as it turned out, one fated to be undone by injuries — most notably to Walker himself.

As the season approached, almost everyone was fascinated by a single aspect:

"The national collegiate football championship," wrote syndicated columnist Bob Considine, "will be decided in the Cotton Bowl on the afternoon of December 3, when unbeaten Notre Dame goes against unbeaten SMU before 75,000 customers."

Continuing, he noted that the game was already sold out "and all the Dallas hotel rooms booked," and that it would be "the regular-season swan song of Doak Walker, one of the nicest and best football players we've ever had. Doak gets as much fan mail as a top movie star, but he remains as normal as they come.

"This modest son of the assistant superintendent of schools of Dallas is a good scholar, gives full credit for his fame to his great blockers, predicts that backfield mate Kyle Rote will be a top fellow, never misses church on the day after a game, and teaches Sunday school.

"P.S. — he's headed for the Philadelphia Eagles."

Notwithstanding the erroneous information at the end, this pretty much encapsulated America's view of Walker. Whatever problems SMU might have, he would fix them — and if any mortal could withstand the mighty machine that was Notre Dame, it was "The Doaker."

In anticipation of this, Matty Bell managed to schedule eight games at home in the Cotton Bowl, where the Mustangs played before an average of 60,617 fans.

The conference stepped off smartly, with Texas burying Texas Tech, 43-0, and TCU smashing usually tough Kansas, 28-0.

The following week, Rice opened by crunching Clemson's 15-game winning streak, 33-7. Rote threw for 180 yards and Gerald Weatherly intercepted three Tiger passes.

In Fort Worth, Oklahoma A&M held leads of 19-0 and 33-14 against TCU, but couldn't hold on. In the final 22 minutes, Lindy Berry drove TCU to a 33-33 deadlock and had the Frogs sitting at the Cowboys' 2-yard line when the game ended.

Berry (22 of 33 attempts for 270 yards) hit Snake Bailey (12 catches for 150 yards) for 15 yards to the A&M three with 20 seconds left, but big John Morton made only a yard in two cracks from there, and the guests escaped defeat.

Overall, the Frogs threw for 333 yards and held a 409-303 total yardage edge, but the tie was a disappointment.

So was SMU's 13-7 victory over Wake Forest for Mustang fans among the 51,000 at the opener who were expecting another opening-game blitz a la 1947 and '48. But the Deacons were a tough bunch — blocking a Walker punt to set up an early score and holding the Ponies to 85 yards on the ground.

Fortunately, Walker could still throw — for 216 yards — and it was enough for a win. He got the Mustangs on the board in the second period with a two-play drive consisting of passes of 42 and 30 yards to Milam, then threw 51 yards to McKissack for the winning score in the third quarter. SMU drove to the Wake Forest 12 late in the game but ran out of time.

AMERICA'S FAVORITE COVER BOY

Next came a 28-27 triumph over Missouri that wasn't quite as wild as the score, since the Tigers' final touchdown came with only 20 seconds left. With no two-point conversion rule, they could only kick the point and close the gap to one.

It was still a fairly brisk ride, as 58,000 watched SMU roll to a pair of 14-point leads before the fourth-quarter Tiger rally. Walker scored three TD's and kicked four extra points to lead the Mustangs, who held a 350-305 edge in total yards. They got 281 of that on the ground, with Walker and Rote contributing 202.

The game was mildly billed as a "revenge" opportunity against the only team that had beaten SMU during the 1947-48 seasons, and both teams displayed spirited attacks. Walker scored the winning touchdown in the third quarter when he smacked at the left side of the line, bounced back, and then circled the end for 19 yards.

It left the Mustangs with their customary 2-0 record, but it would be the last time SMU would stand undefeated in Walker's career.

Elsewhere around the league, anguish prevailed.

Rice suffered what would be its only defeat of the season (13-7 to LSU), Texas had four starters hobbling on bad knees on the eve of the Oklahoma game, and Dutch Meyer was fuming over a 27-7 loss in Fayetteville.

Estimating that Arkansas had run "no more than six or seven legal plays," Meyer protested the game to league officials. Of particular note, he said, was the way the Hog offensive linemen used their elbows, one of which had broken the jaw of TCU's Orein Browning.

As if on cue, several other outposts joined Meyer in his condemnation of the Hogs, and tales of foul treatment in the hills were brought to light. It was even suggested that the Razorbacks might fit better in another league.

During the first week in October, SMU enjoyed its unbeaten status through an idle week, while Rice got well against New Mexico, 55-0, TCU won at Indiana, 13-6, and Oklahoma edged Texas, 20-14, in a game where the total yardage was 257-249. The Longhorns doomed themselves

Doak rushed for 2,076 yards and passed for 1,786 yards, scored a school-record 303 points and punted for a 39.6-yard average at SMU.

early, however, with mistakes.

In the national headline game, one of the most powerful teams in Army history rolled into Ann Arbor and smashed Michigan's 25-game winning streak with a 21-7 victory, before a stunned audience of 97,000.

It established the Cadets as the logical challenger to Notre Dame for the right to claim the national championship, but unfortunately, the historic series between the two great powers had ended in 1947. So at the end of the season, they both remained unbeaten and averaging better than 35 points a game, and the nation was left wondering.

During the following week, however, there was no doubt in Matty Bell's mind about SMU's immediate fate. Having predicted at the start of the season that the Mustangs would lose four times, he identified the upcoming Rice game as the first of the losses. He was proven a sad prophet on both counts.

"I don't see how SMU can beat Rice with that senior team," he said. "It has speed, passing, running, outweighs us, has more experience, and the players made a pledge before the season started that they'd win the conference championship."

On October 15, wearing the imposing solid blue battle dress of the Jess Neely era, Rice arrived at the Cotton Bowl, tipped its hat to 72,000 witnesses, and shattered forever the myth of the "invincible" Mustangs.

It was a game that fit the worst nightmare of the SMU fan: the Mustangs lost their first conference game since 1946, and Walker went down with a serious injury.

As the evening began, however, the game had an old, familiar look to it. After Rice failed to capitalize on a fumble recovery, SMU drove 75 yards, with Payne hitting Rote on a 51-yard scoring pass. On their next possession, the Mustangs drove 86 yards, with Walker throwing to Milam for a 14-0 lead.

Rice had cut it to 14-6 by halftime, but it still looked like SMU's game.

It began to change abruptly, however, when Rice's Sonny Wyatt came sailing out of the chute with the second-half kickoff, 36 yards to the 47.

From there, the Owls drove to a touchdown — then pulled off an onside kick and drove to another. The Mustangs' lead had evaporated, and they still hadn't handled the

In 1949, with Doak injured for two games, the Mustangs slipped to a 5-4-1 record.

ball in the second half. When they did, disaster struck — Rice turned an 80-yard interception return into a 27-14 lead.

On the following SMU drive, Walker swept around end for a short gain and then relaxed as he went out of bounds.

But Rice defender Gerald Weatherly slammed into Walker with a tackle that sent both of them hurtling into the metal wheelchair of a war veteran who was watching the game from the sideline. The SMU star suffered a facial cut and was knocked woozy with a concussion.

For SMU fans, the horrifying sight of Walker lying motionless on the ground eventually became the freeze-frame for a season gone south — but it was actually the least of three physical problems that sidelined him for all or part of five games.

The Rice encounter was the first of these, and although

Walker returned after five minutes to call plays and provide inspiration, he did not run or throw for the remainder. The final was 41-27, Rice.

Typically, Walker sought out Weatherly after the game to say that he realized the hit was unintentional, and they shook hands.

In the national headliner that week, Notre Dame overwhelmed Tulane, the eventual Southeastern Conference champion, 46-7. A few days later, a national columnist warned the Irish that if this behavior continued, they would find it difficult to schedule future opponents.

Painful though Walker's injury had been, he got hit at midweek by something far worse — the flu.

By Thursday, he was in a hospital bed, and SMU coaches were assured that he would be unavailable for the next game. This was against Kentucky, a top-10 team that was 5-0 and had outscored its foes, 206-7.

"Aw, there's no point in us even practicing this week," said Moanin' Matty.

It turned out, however, to be quite a week.

In Fort Worth, in another SWC-SEC matchup, John Dottley contributed scoring runs of 59 and 68 yards to a 506-yard Ole Miss assault, but Berry brought the Frogs back from a two-touchdown deficit with three scoring passes in a 33-27 triumph.

In Austin, Texas nearly ran Rice out of Memorial Stadium in a first half during which the Longhorns built a 9-1 advantage in first downs and a 15-0 lead.

But for the second consecutive week, the class of the Owls showed in the second half, when they marched downfield on three long drives behind second-string quarterback Vernon Glass. As time expired, Froggie Williams booted a dramatic 28-yard field goal and the Owls — with a 17-15 win — were rolling toward the Cotton Bowl.

And in Dallas, SMU's anonymous army marched out of the shadows and knocked off a giant.

Although the supposed "Win One for Doak" crusade was essentially a press fantasy, the Mustangs played an inspired game against a big, tough team with a future all-American (Babe Parilli) at quarterback that was headed for the Sugar Bowl.

Rote, McKissack and Champion led a ground attack that picked up 206 yards and fueled scoring drives of 65, 88 and 73 yards, with "Killer Kyle" scoring twice in a 20-7 win. The other score came on a 49-yard pass from Benners to Rusty Russell Jr., and the Mustangs were at the Kentucky 7 when the game ended.

Facing a fired-up SMU defense, Kentucky lost three fumbles, while Folsom intercepted a pass and made an open-field tackle to save a touchdown.

Despite all this, Wildcat coach Paul (Bear) Bryant said he was most impressed with referee Ray McCulloch, who he blamed for swinging the game SMU's way. Penalty yardage was actually even, but the 'Cats had a touchdown called back.

"I'd rather have that referee on my team than any of my players," rasped the Bear, graciously.

Another powerhouse in distress, North Carolina, suggested after a 13-7 loss in Baton Rouge that LSU had

watered down its field to slow Tar Heel all-American Choo-Choo Justice.

Unmoved, Tiger Athletic Director T.P. Heard replied, "We would have won that game on concrete."

And Tulane announced that, after due consideration of all factors involved, it had decided to drop the Notre Dame series after the 1950 game in New Orleans.

As the Mustangs prepared to face Texas, Walker was released from the hospital and cleared to play, although he was still wobbly.

He played, in fact, less than a quarter. But of course, he won the game.

It was the third in a series of bitter defeats for the Longhorns, who lost a fumble at the SMU three, saw another drive stall at the 10, and watched their super receiver, Ben Procter, drop a pass in the end zone with 20 seconds remaining.

Their only score came on a one-yard runback of an interception of a deflected Benners pass in the third quarter. But Blakely stormed through to block the conversion attempt, and SMU awakened.

Rolling down the field behind the passing of Rote and Benners, the Mustangs reached the Texas 20 as time expired in the third quarter.

On the first play of the final period, Rote took a five-yard pass from Benners near the sideline and ran through three Longhorns en route to the goal line. Walker, who had played sparingly, came in and kicked the extra point, and SMU hung on to win, 7-6, in front of a sellout crowd of 75,000.

A few days later, an AP writer did identical interviews with Justice and Walker about the prospect of facing Notre Dame later in the year; the essential query being: "are you afraid?"

"Why no," said SMU's all-American boy, "it wouldn't be right to be afraid of anyone."

Equally typical was his response when asked what made him so good: "The other 10 guys."

Unfortunately for SMU, the Aggies were also feeling fearless that week.

Having gone winless (but tying Texas) in 1948, the Ags were having a similar year in '49 — they came in with a sparkling 1-6 record, having defeated Texas Tech and been flattened by everyone else.

It was assumed that 31,000 showed up at Kyle Field to watch the Mustangs, favored by three touchdowns. Or possibly to be on hand in case A&M scored — something it hadn't done at home all year.

The hard-pressed Aggies were, among other things, playing with a 188-pound offensive guard named Carl Molberg — who looked across at his SMU foe on the game's first snap and said, "This is going to be interesting."

When the SMU player asked him why, Molberg replied, "because this is our eighth game, and you're the first guy I've played against who is anywhere near my size."

Though still underweight, Walker was definitely his old self as he and Rote combined for 234 yards on the day and drove SMU relentlessly to a 20-6 halftime lead. The Aggies had scored, but they hadn't managed much else.

But with Bob Smith running through the Mustangs for 175 yards, the second half was another story. A&M mounted two third-quarter drives and tied the score.

The deadlock lasted for as long as it took Rote to return the ensuing kickoff 100 yards for a seven-point SMU lead. It looked secure through most of the final period, and then disaster struck the Ponies.

Walker and Rote misfired on a handoff, and A&M recovered the loose ball at the Mustang 30. A drive was promptly underway that tied the score at 27-27 — and that's the way it ended.

This mortifying event ensured that SMU — which in 1947-48 had become the first non-wartime team in SWC history to win back-to-back undisputed titles — would not win a third.

All of which was scant solace to the Arkansas Razorbacks — who came trotting into the Cotton Bowl just in time to be transformed into roast suckling pig.

For the first time since the Missouri game, the Mustangs looked like the team that had been renowned from coast-to-coast for two seasons, as they scored three times in the first quarter and trampled the Hogs, 34-6.

They finished with 19 first downs and 417 total yards — of which 211 belonged to Walker. He had also scored three times and flipped a TD pass to Champion.

It raised SMU to 5-1-1 on the year, with prospects still

good for an outstanding season.

But in the remarkable time that has ever since been known simply as "The Doak Walker Era," it was to be their final victory.

Meanwhile, in Austin, two teams that had had back-to-back encounters with Baylor — revived under Bob Woodruff — met to compare notes. Two weeks earlier, TCU had tossed the Bears nine interceptions and been rudely eliminated from title contention in a 40-14 rout. The following week, Texas had played its best game of the year, blanking the undefeated Bruins, 20-0.

Mathematicians from Wichita to Kursk had this one figured. And Dutch Meyer fooled 'em all.

Throwing a nine-man line at the Longhorns and stuffing the normally pass-happy attack in their pocket, the Frogs repeatedly sacked UT quarterback Paul Campbell, cut Berry loose on a 33-yard scoring run, and upset their chagrined hosts, 14-13.

As the emotional Meyer stood savoring the victory afterward, Snake Bailey walked by and tossed him the game ball.

"This one's for you, Coach," he said.

On the same day in New York, Notre Dame crushed North Carolina, 42-6. Playing valiantly without the injured Justice, the Tar Heels finished the first half tied, 6-6, but were rolled under in the final 30 minutes as they managed only 89 yards to 518 by the Fighting Irish.

The following week, 63,000 arrived in the Cotton Bowl to watch the rejuvenated Mustangs do their stuff. Although Baylor came in at 7-1 and SMU's mangled defense was obviously struggling, the Ponies were favored by at least a touchdown in most projections.

This perception began to disappear on the game's first play, when Adrian Burk dropped back and launched a towering heave that was estimated to have traveled 55 yards in the air before Dudley Parker ran under it at the SMU 35 and raced goalward to complete an 80-yard scoring play.

It was a special play called by Baylor offensive coordinator Frank Broyles, and after that, the Mustangs were never really in the game. They trailed, 21-6, at the half and never moved closer than nine points thereafter, trailing by 16 throughout most of the second half. Walker caught a touchdown pass lying on his back in the end zone with eight seconds left to make the final score, 35-26, but it was a sad affair.

Walker and Rote both had good days offensively, and SMU totaled 370 yards, but the defense surrendered more than 400. One Baylor score came after Walker, desperate to keep pace with the Bear scoring machine, gambled on fourth and 10 from the SMU 46 and threw incomplete.

It marked the third time in eight games that the Mustangs had scored four times and failed to win. Worse, Walker had pulled up lame late in the game with what would prove a career-ending injury — a "charley horse" that kept getting worse.

A far more thrilling affair unfolded in Fort Worth, where Rice rode Tobin Rote's passes to Froggie Williams to a 20-0 halftime lead, then hung on for dear life as Berry — wearing a plaster mask to protect a broken jaw suffered in the Texas game — launched another flaming comeback.

This one eventually fell short, as Rice won, 20-14. But it required luck and last-minute heroics from defensive back Rex Procter.

With Rice never advancing beyond its 46 in the second half, the Frogs constantly paraded goalward, scoring twice and once being halted at the one-yard line. Late in the game, Dan Wilde raced toward the end zone with what could have been the "upset" touchdown, but Procter knocked him out of bounds at the two, after a 27-yard journey.

From there, Berry scored, but it was nullified by a backfield-in-motion penalty. Then he threw an apparent TD pass to George Boal, who was one step beyond the end line.

A fourth-down pass failed and Rice held — but moments later Berry was whizzing back upfield on a 44-yard punt return, and Proctor was forced to rescue Rice again with an interception at the five just before time expired.

This left TCU and SMU facing a final battle with two wounded stars, and the Bears and Owls slated for a title showdown in Houston. But Rice had absorbed the last great challenge to its power, and would not be stressed again.

As the final SWC weekend approached, Texas and A&M resumed their elegant rivalry, with the Aggies staging a raid on a Longhorn bonfire. In the confusion, the raiders' car was abandoned after it caught fire, and a Texas guard was injured when one of his fraternity brothers mistook him for an Aggie and hit him over the head with a club.

The festivities continued during the game — won by the Longhorns, 42-14 — when Smith, the Aggies' star fullback, was decked by Texas end Ray Stone and missed the entire third quarter.

In Houston, Rice spotted Baylor a touchdown and then rolled over the Bears, 21-7, to win the conference championship. A month later, they would bury Justice and North Carolina in a 27-13 Cotton Bowl victory in which Jess Neely called off the dogs with a four-touchdown lead entering the final period.

And in Fort Worth, a capacity crowd of 33,000 turned out to watch Walker and Berry duel for the last time. Some, perhaps, had read a report that the SMU star was "limping," but it added that he was expected to play 60 minutes.

Berry was about to conclude a career in which he played in 41 consecutive games — the final two wearing that grotesque plaster mask. In this one, it didn't prevent him from throwing for 250 yards.

It was also the final duel between Dutch Meyer and Matty Bell. There had been rumors — which he milked for all they were worth in a tearful pre-game speech — that Dutch would be replaced, while Matty had already decided to retire after the Notre Dame game the following week.

There was no title on the line, but it turned out to be the most momentous of the week's engagements.

Despite his injury, Walker broke for a 27-yard run on an SMU scoring drive in the first quarter, which Rote climaxed by storming 37 yards through assorted Frogs to the end zone.

In the second quarter, Berry retaliated with a 56-yard pass to George Boal followed by a 29-yard scoring pass to Jimmy Hickey. In the third quarter, he capped a 51-yard drive with a short plunge over the goal line, but the Mustangs struck back on Benners' 57-yard TD pass to Rusty Russell Jr. Rote, who had 162 tandem yards for the day, missed the extra point, leaving the Frogs up, 14-13.

In the final period, Berry drove the Frogs 80 yards and hit Jack Archer with the TD pass that clinched a 21-13 win — TCU's first over the Mustangs in seven years.

But the day's most crucial event had occurred early in the third quarter, when a long SMU drive was halted at the

TCU 18. Near midfield, Walker moved through a gap in the line and was hit hard on his injured leg by TCU's Orein Browning — playing his first game since his jaw was broken against Arkansas.

"The leg was getting worse," Walker recalls, "but we were driving for a go-ahead touchdown, so Matty put me back in and said, 'Don't carry the ball.'

"But I took the snap on a pass play, and that hole opened, and I couldn't resist. Just a stupid play."

And so, late in the afternoon, there was a collision in the middle of TCU Stadium between a lame superstar and a player who had missed nearly the entire year with a broken jaw ... and the greatest career in the history of the Southwest Conference came to an end.

In what amounted to slightly better than half a season, Walker had accumulated 1,054 yards in total offense, finished fourth in the nation in scoring (83 points) and fifth in punting (42.1) and become the only three-time consensus all-American the SWC would ever have (Texas' Hub Bechtol was all-American three times, twice consensus).

By this time, a massive steel strike had finally been settled, the Red Army had marched into Chungking, and the great circus ape, Gargantua, had died.

But the real Gargantua was on its way to the Cotton Bowl — a Notre Dame team that had not lost in four years.

Within that span, the Fighting Irish, coached by Frank Leahy, produced 17 all-Americans, two Heisman Trophy winners and three national champions. The 1949 team was considered the best of the lot, and was probably responsible — more than any other group since the Four Horsemen teams — for perpetuating the image of Notre Dame as a perennially invincible juggernaut.

The Fighting Irish had swept aside nine opponents without breaking a sweat en route to a 10-0 season, in which they outscored their foes 360-86. There was an all-America quarterback (Bob Williams), an all-America tackle (Jim Martin), and an all-America fullback who carried his rushing average in his nickname: Emil (Six-Yard) Sitko.

Worst of all, there was a 6-foot-4, 245-pound behemoth named Leon Hart, a two-way end who would become the last lineman in history to win the Heisman Trophy. On game day, Notre Dame was favored by 27 1/2 points.

But the Fighting Irish were nearly undone by Rote —

who had the greatest game of his career — and an adversary they never saw, a retired former TCU assistant named Mike Brumbelow. Bell, a close friend, enlisted him to travel to several Notre Dame games during the fall and scout the team. The week of the game, he showed up in Dallas with his notes.

"It was the most extensive scouting report I ever saw," says Rote, who subsequently played 12 years with the New York Giants. "It was better than anything I ever saw in the NFL, and by the end of the week, anything Mike said, we believed it."

With the information provided by Brumbelow, Russell charted an offense designed to neutralize Notre Dame's size advantage (20 pounds per man) by "spreading the game from sideline to sideline" just as he had done in the 30's at Masonic Home. Hence, the spread.

In the pre-game dressing room, the Mustangs were confronted by raw emotion: dressed in street clothes, choking back tears, Doak Walker told them it had been his lifelong dream to play against Notre Dame. Now, he never would — but they could.

In a sudden surge, the Mustangs poured through the dressing room door — all except one. At that moment, Rote approached Bell and said, "Don't worry, Coach, we won't let you down," and then held out his hand. When Bell grasped it, he got a shock — Rote had an electric buzzer concealed in his palm.

"I still can't explain why I did it," Rote says, " but as soon as I saw the look on his face, I wished I hadn't."

Stationed at tailback in the spread, Rote — noted primarily for his running — completed three passes on SMU's first drive, and a pattern was established.

For the remainder of the game, Rote would sweep right or left on the run-pass option, and the bedeviled Irish defense was forced to lie back and wait. The effectiveness was further enhanced by slant blocking from the Mustangs, which cut down the Notre Dame rush.

This latter tactic led to an amazing match: the job of blocking Hart fell to the smallest Mustang on the field, 145-pound wingback Johnny Champion, who was instructed to aim for the ankles. It worked well enough, except for a couple of instances in which he was forced to tackle his huge adversary.

"I lost the game for us. Just as I threw the ball, out of the corner of my eye I saw Champion all alone in the end zone. I can still see him today ..."

Kyle Rote

That ceased after Hart finally inquired, pleasantly, if Champion planned to live through the afternoon. Champion's blocking, however, was a key factor.

When the day was finished, Rote would score three times and accumulate 261 yards: 115 rushing and 146 passing.

Nevertheless, Notre Dame put together two touchdown drives and led, 13-0, at the half.

The Irish had been burned once, when Champion took a handoff from Rote on a reverse and threw to Zohn Milam on a play that carried 78 yards to the Notre Dame 6. But on fourth down, Rote was stopped inches from the goal line.

In the third quarter, Rote scored at the end of a 62-yard drive, cutting it to 13-7. Notre Dame retaliated, and it was a 20-7 game when the fourth period opened.

Suddenly, SMU struck again, as Rote hit Champion for 68 yards to the Irish one-yard line, then scored on the next play. Quickly, the Mustangs were back after a Champion punt return, and Rote tied it at 20. Linebacker Jerry Groom, a thorn in SMU's side all day, blocked the extra-point attempt.

Then, Rote says, "Notre Dame showed its class" by rolling almost easily downfield, with halfback Billy Barrett

scoring from the six. With six minutes left, it seemed that the Irish — finally — had won.

Hardly. Alternating Rote's runs with Benners' passes, the Mustangs swept downfield one last time, 67 yards until they stood, again, in the shadow of the Irish goal.

But from the four, Rote's jump pass for Blakely in the end zone was intercepted by Groom, and it was finally over.

"I lost the game for us," Rote says. "Just as I threw the ball, out of the corner of my eye I saw Champion all alone in the end zone. I can still see him today ..."

But, after reaffirming that this had been the greatest team he had ever coached, Leahy was soon calling Rote "the most underrated player in America." In 1950, Rote was a consensus all-American and finished second in the Heisman voting.

Afterward, the Notre Dame locker room was visited by the other SMU tailback — Walker — who was greeted by a standing ovation and obliged to make a short speech.

And 25 years later, Rote received an invitation to a reunion of the '49 Notre Dame team — as an honorary member.

"I've been to several of their reunions since, and I get the newsletter regularly," he says. "They are gentlemen, one and all, and I have thoroughly enjoyed the friendship."

The game marked the end of a remarkable era, one that began with a nondescript team losing half its games in a 23,000-seat stadium ... and ended with 75,000 on their feet, cheering an amazing team that — even with its star sitting on the bench — had learned to play a different game.

Preserved in the Fireside Book of Football is the following passage, filed by Bert McGrane of The Des Moines Register-Tribune:

"Notre Dame won, 27-20, but it was SMU's indomitable array that dashed away, chins high, at the finish, with most of the 75,457 customers who jammed the Cotton Bowl still roaring a Mustang tribute that began with the kickoff and hasn't ended yet.

"This was a hair-lifting, breathtaking uprising by an underdog team that positively could not have made a better effort."

"I think," Rote says, laughing, "that in a sense, we felt we were representing all the underdogs in the world. I think many others may also have perceived us that way."

CHAPTER NINE

Doak & SMU vs. the Frogs: A 3-Year War

SMU and TCU tied, 19–19 and 7-7, in 1947 and 1948. In 1949, TCU finally broke the "SMU Jinx" with a 21-13 win.

As their distinctly competitive relationship stood on the eve of its final episode, Doak Walker had finally reduced Dutch Meyer to tears.

Or so it seemed on November 26, 1949, a day when two brilliant collegiate careers came to a close and one went into temporary hiding.

As a backdrop, a capacity crowd of 33,000 filed into TCU Stadium to view the last of three memorable duels between Walker and TCU's Lindy Berry — a pair of opposing tailbacks who amassed more than 8,000 total yards in their careers, not to mention about 2,000 in punt returns.

It was also to be the last meeting ever between two old pals and fierce rivals — TCU's Meyer and SMU's Matty Bell, who had announced that he would retire after the Mustangs' final game the following week against Notre Dame.

They had been coaching companions two decades earlier and remained off-season pals and fishing buddies. But since the mid-1930's, they had been adversaries in a heated rivalry that, of late, had not gone well for the Frogs — who had last beaten the Ponies in 1942.

Oh, there had been two momentous upsets in 1947 and '48, when underdog TCU teams led by Berry had played Cotton Bowl-bound SMU teams to 19-19 and 7-7 ties. But the very nature of those games had only added to Meyer's frustration.

Each time, despite a brilliant performance by Berry, Walker had engineered last-minute drives enabling SMU to escape defeat — the last one having also cost Dutch a perfectly good hat.

As for the opposing stars, it was a final clash of eagles — but this time there was no title on the line and both were a bit the worse for wear.

Walker was hobbled by a severe thigh bruise and Berry — playing his 41st consecutive game as a Frog — was wearing a plaster mask protecting a broken jaw.

But these ailments paled in comparison to the wounded heart of Dutch Meyer — a sad, forlorn sight as he entered the TCU dressing room.

"We were all gathered in there waiting for him," Berry says, "and finally here he comes — kind of shuffling around and mumbling, and gettin' weepy, and just looking like he was about to start blubbering.

"Finally, he starts talking, and he says, 'Well boys, I ... I guess, I guess this is gonna be my last game,' and his voice started cracking, and he says, 'They ... they haven't ... renewed my contract ... so I guess this is it for me.'

"Then he looks up at us, with tears streaming down his face, and he says, 'Boy, I sure would love to beat Matty one more time!'

"Well, I was the captain, so I held a quick team meeting and I told 'em, 'Look, we've just got to go out there and win this game for Dutch,' and everybody agreed and we went out all fired up."

The two teams were pretty evenly matched, anyway — both severely battered by injuries but still potent offensively. Again, Berry was brilliant — amassing 250 total yards, scoring once and throwing for two TD's as the Frogs finally broke the "SMU Jinx" with a 21-13 victory.

The win almost was assured to the Frogs in the third quarter when Walker took a hit on his bad leg and left the game for good. It turned out to be the last play of his glittering career, as the leg failed to get well the next week and he missed the Notre Dame game.

The win boosted TCU to 6-3-1 on the year and Berry — the valiant star perpetually overshadowed by the famous Mustang — finished with 4,452 career yards, about

"Well, I was the captain, so I held a quick team meeting and I told 'em, 'Look, we've just got to go out there and win this game for Dutch,' and everybody agreed and we went out all fired up."

Lindy Berry

600 more than Walker.

At the end, Meyer cried again. So did Mr. and Mrs. Charles Berry, who watched their son play one of his finest games in his last performance. Walker limped out to the middle of the field, hugged Berry and congratulated him.

In the dressing room, Dutch was rather coy with reporters about the abrupt demise of his career.

"A little while later," Berry says, laughing, "we found out that two days before the SMU game, he had signed a new three-year contract."

In the late 1940's, however, any ruse was deemed acceptable in the continuing crusade to stop Doak Walker.

"He was just so damn spectacular," says James (Froggie) Williams, the formidable Rice end who was the SWC's other consensus all-American in 1949.

"He always seemed to do the right thing at the right time," Williams says. "He was like that Frank Merriwell guy, in cleats.

"It seemed like, those three years (1947, '48 and '49), our whole game plan was, 'Don't let Doak run up and down the field and beat you' — but the first two years (14-0 and 33-7 SMU wins) we didn't do a very good job of it."

But by 1949, coach Jess Neely's Owls were ready. It was one of the strongest teams in SWC history, with a crowd of running backs, a large contingent of seniors including Williams, quarterback Tobin Rote and all-America center Joe Watson, and one of the deadliest offensive lines ever assembled.

Plus a mission.

"By the time we came to the Cotton Bowl (October 15)," Williams says, "we'd been playing SMU for six weeks.

"They called us the 'Vow Team' because we had all taken a vow to win the championship. We had had strong teams in 1947 and '48 (after a co-championship in '46) but at times we hadn't played well. In '48, especially, we were disappointed in the season we had.

"So we came back ready to win a title, and we knew we would have the strongest team, along with probably Texas. But the other half of our vow was SMU.

"Jess was a great coach and an extremely strong personality, and losing bothered him. The way he coached, we would run a scrimmage every day in practice. And every day that year, we played SMU.

"We knew there was no way we could lose the game — if we could stop Walker."

As it turned out, the Owls won the game and stopped Walker — both in dramatic fashion.

In the early going, it looked like a replay of previous years, with SMU scoring on two long touchdown drives to take a 14-0 lead. But the Owls scored late in the half and three times in quick succession in the third quarter to take a 27-14 lead.

At that point, linebacker Gerald Weatherly hit Walker as he went out of bounds and crashed him into a wheelchair, giving him a slight concussion.

Although Walker returned to the game, he never carried the ball again. Rice won, 41-27, handing SMU its first conference defeat in three years.

Doak rams through the middle of the Texas A&M defense for a TD in 1949. The game ended in a 27-27 tie.

"Well, let me explain something about that hit," Williams says. "I know a lot of people got upset about it, but Gerald wasn't trying to hit him with a cheap shot out of bounds.

"One of the things Doak did better than anyone I ever saw was use the sideline like a tightrope. There were a lot of people who thought they had him forced out of bounds and eased up, and he'd dart down that line and go past 'em — and he hurt us bad that way the previous year.

DOAK & SMU vs. TCU: A 3-YEAR WAR

"So we were all told not to ease up and give him the sideline, and that's how that hit occurred.

"The other thing about that play was that it didn't cost them the game; we were already ahead and getting stronger."

The following week in Austin, the Owls spotted Texas a 15-0 halftime lead and then came back to win, 17-15, on Williams' dramatic field goal as time expired.

"People always ask me about that field goal," he says, "but what won it for us was the way our offensive line just shoved them back in the second half. And changing quarterbacks.

"Tobin became famous as a brilliant pro quarterback, of course, but in college he was somewhat erratic. He was fantastic against SMU, but cold as ice against Texas. We were used to his streaks by then, however, and we told Jess, 'Don't be afraid to put Vernon Glass in, because we can win with him.'

"That's what Jess did in the second half, and when Vernon came into the huddle, our line gave him four plays to run and told him to stick to 'em.

"The second half, we just kept running those four plays right through Texas, because we knew they couldn't handle our offensive line."

As dramatic as the Texas win was, however, Williams says it was the SMU game that turned Rice (10-1) into the fifth-ranked team in the country.

"Our season turned on that game," he says, "because SMU had been so dominant, and Doak Walker so unbeatable. In that game, we proved ourselves.

"One of the things people didn't realize about him until they played him once was how hard he was to bring down. He was strong and tough, and he didn't go down just because you laid a lick on him. Very hard to tackle.

"But the main thing was this: Doak could hurt you throwing the ball, but not near as bad as he could running with it on pass plays. So many times he beat people on plays like that — he'd fade back and get you spread out all over the field, then he'd take off running.

"After that, you had to try him one-on-one, and that was not a good ratio.

"So Jess moved us out of that wide-tackle six and into a five-man line and said, 'If he wants to throw, let him.

Don't rush him — but don't let him run.' "

Dressed in solid blue and devoted to hat-on-hat football, Neely's Owls in those days were usually an awesome sight.

"The defense we used against North Carolina in the Cotton Bowl was a seven diamond," Williams says. "Jess liked to always put a guy right over the center, and if things went well it was a real good way to disrupt an offense.

"He had another thing he liked to do — if we had the ball to open the game. It was kinda like a flying wedge — just give the ball to the fullback and everyone converge on the center of the line. Sort of an intimidation thing.

"He had some great quarterbacks, like Tobin, but Jess Neely, I'll tell you, was going to run the damn football."

But for two years, nothing the Owls tried worked against SMU. The tide turned in 1949, when the Owls were strong and the Mustangs were wounded.

And at the end, Berry and Williams — two stars who spent their careers chasing Walker — found themselves, like him, specatators at the Notre Dame game.

"Someone gave me a ticket," Berry says, "so I went over to see it, and I have always been glad — because it was one of the greatest games I ever saw."

Williams came up from Houston for the game, with a ticket someone gave him.

"Funny," he says. "Seems like all my career at Rice, we just tried to concentrate on beating Doak Walker, and we almost never did. It was kind of like an obsession.

"But sitting there in the Cotton Bowl that day, I started cheering for those danged Mustangs.

"And looking back, I have to admit I am unabashedly a fan of Doak Walker. I honestly believe he was born to run that spread offense of Rusty Russell's, and he did it magnificently.

"I don't want to hear any statistics about somebody who just runs the ball and gains 2,000 yards. They're not playing the same game he was — both ways, 60 minutes, thinking up a half-dozen different ways to beat you. He was a great player who always came through in the clutch.

"I have seen a lot of football, and a lot of players. I have never seen anyone who was the equal of Doak Walker."

103

Once, When the Lions Roared in the NFL

n December 3, 1949, Doak Walker's final act as an SMU Mustang was to visit the Notre Dame locker room and congratulate the Fighting Irish — who hailed him as if he had thrown the winning touchdown pass.

And when, speaking on behalf of his storied legion, Frank Leahy told Walker how much they regretted not have had the honor of competing against him, he replied, simply, "I couldn't have done any better today than Kyle Rote did."

And so, once again, modesty prevailed.

The achievements of the "Doak Walker Era," however, were hardly modest.

In 35 games at SMU, Walker had rushed for 2,076 yards, passed for 1,786, caught passes for 475, returned punts for 750 (15.0 average), kickoffs for 756 (29.1), punted 85 times for a 39.6 average, intercepted 12 passes and scored 303 points.

He had been four times all-conference, three times an all-American, won the Heisman and Maxwell awards, and graced the cover of 47 magazines.

SMU, a small-enrollment private school that only four years earlier had been thrilled with crowds of 23,000, was now filling a 75,000-seat coliseum that had been expanded twice to handle the overflow. The Mustangs would continue to draw well there for a decade — until the arrival of pro football in 1960 would begin to erode the popularity of the college game.

The eyes of the nation had been cast upon the Southwest Conference, where a wide-open and generally pass-oriented style captured the attention and imagination of fans from coast-to-coast — and the league entered a final

"Golden Era" prior to a long slide into oblivion.

Much of this was due to the fact that opponents simply could never predict what Walker might do next. This time, however, his next move seemed obvious: pro ball.

Actually his next move came on March 17, 1950, when he and Norma Peterson, the beautiful SMU coed he had dated for three years, were married.

By this time, he had received sage advice on his choice of careers from Dr. Eddie Anderson, who had coached him in the College All-Star game.

Anderson advised the slight (5-11, 165) SMU star to pack up immediately following the game, "go home, and forget about pro football before you get hurt. You're too small to play that game."

Raleigh Blakely recalls reading Anderson's advice in the newspaper.

"I couldn't believe it," he says. "A three-time all-Ameri-

ONCE, WHEN THE LIONS ROARED

During six seasons in Detroit, Doak and Bobby Layne (left) led the Lions to two NFL titles.

can, Heisman Trophy winner, a guy who had done everything possible in his career, and this coach was saying he wasn't good enough to play?"

Anderson was actually a kindly gent, trying to offer helpful advice, possibly prevent the loss of life or limb, and do the lad a good turn.

He was also dead wrong.

As a National Football League rookie with Detroit in 1950, Walker led the Lions in kickoff returns and led the league in scoring with 128 points — only 10 off the all-time record then held by Don Hutson.

At the end of the season he was named All-Pro and received a letter from Anderson admitting his mistake.

He had also taken part in the first step of a rejuvenation that ushered in a golden era for the Lions — who after years of mediocrity would win four Western Conference

titles and three NFL championships between 1952 and 1957.

The coaches who directed this victorious surge were Buddy Parker and George Wilson — but the man who started it was Bo McMillin, who with a slight nudge had the presence of mind to reunite Walker and Bobby Layne.

McMillin and Matty Bell had been teammates at Fort Worth's North Side High School and later with Centre College's "Prayin' Colonels," — a small-college juggernaut that gained lasting fame with a 6-0 upset that snapped Harvard's 25-game winning streak in 1921.

Through long coaching careers, they remained close friends, and when Walker finished his SMU career, Matty got a call from Bo.

"At that time," Walker says, "Detroit had the draft rights to me, and Bo contacted Matty and asked if I could help them. They had acquired the draft rights in 1948, when they finished last and had the first pick. So they took me as a future, but they could have changed it in '49.

"Matty told him that if he could make a trade and get me and Bobby on the team together, he could win a championship."

By that time, Layne had spent two seasons as a pro — one with a strong team that didn't need him, and one with a team on its way to historical footnote status.

"When Bobby got out of Texas, he was drafted by the Chicago Bears," Walker says, "but he only stayed there one year (1948). They had Sid Luckman and Johnny Lujack, and he kinda got lost in the shuffle.

"They traded him to the New York Bulldogs — a franchise owned by Kate Smith. It was quite a deal — they played every week hoping her variety show didn't bomb, and then raced each other to the bank in case the paychecks bounced.

"So after talking to Matty, McMillin bought Bobby's contract for $10,000, and he joined the Lions."

Walker, meanwhile, proved as adept at contract negotiations as he was tightroping a sideline, and signed for $24,000, nudging top dollar in the NFL at that time.

The Bulldogs soon became the New York Yankees, then the Dallas Texans, and finally the Baltimore Colts. By that time, Layne and Walker had the Lions roaring.

To make way for the reunited pair, McMillin traded quarterback Frank Tripucka and halfback Bullet Bill Dudley — who had led the '49 Lions in rushing, scoring, punting and punt returns. Their replacements were able, however.

In 1950, Layne threw for 2,300 yards, Walker led the league in scoring, and the other halfback, Bob (Hunchy) Hoernschemeyer, averaged nearly six yards a carry as the Lions went 6-6, their best finish since the war.

Layne, Walker and Hoernschemeyer were part of a sudden influx of talent through trades and the draft that moved the team from the bottom of the standings to the top almost overnight.

"All that was due to Bo McMillin," Walker says. "He started rebuilding that team from the ground up, and did it quickly. He was a really enlightening guy — greatest after-dinner speaker I ever heard — and he could have been the greatest coach ever in Detroit.

"But Bo was a sick man, and that '50 season was the last

Doak races for 16 yards in the Lions' 21-17 loss to San Francisco in the 1951 NFL playoffs.

time he coached us (he died of cancer early in 1952).

"Buddy Parker came in, and we started winning. He was a terrific coach, and I loved the guy. But all the same, those were Bo's players — something like 32 or 33 he brought in. He rebuilt two-thirds of the team in a couple of years."

In 1951, Layne threw for 2,400 yards, Hoernschemeyer averaged better than five yards a carry, Walker scored 97 points and averaged 27.2 on kickoff returns, and the Lions went into the last game of the season with a chance to win the conference title. But they lost to San Francisco, and the Los Angeles Rams went on to win the NFL title against Cleveland.

By now, the fullback was Pat Harder — who had played on an NFL champion with the Cardinals — and other helpful new arrivals included Leon Hart, Yale Lary, Dorne Dibble, Jim Doran, Lou Creekmur, Cloyce Box, Jack Christiansen, Thurman McGraw, LaVern Torgeson and Bob Smith.

And the center of the line was anchored by the old 300-

pound veteran, Les Bingaman.

"A great player, with a brilliant football mind," Walker says. "And for five yards, as fast as anyone on the field.

"He was a great help to me when I first came up, and I learned a lot from him. He would get down in the line and tell guys to move left or move right, and they would. When he got 'em all situated, they were usually in the right place to stop the play.

"He's the one who told me that you could always tell whether I was running to the right or the left because my knuckles turned white when I lined up in a certain stance. So I changed my stance."

By 1952, the Lions were ready to roll off three consecutive conference championships, winning two NFL titles along the way. Walker was sidelined with a hamstring injury much of the season — but returned in time to contribute a 67-yard scoring run in a 17-7 victory over the Browns for the NFL championship.

"That's pretty much the image you have of Doak," says Yale Lary, who punted and played defensive back with the Lions. "About the only thing that stopped him was an injury.

"When I was growing up in Fort Worth (North Side), I saw him play two of the most exciting games I ever saw against TCU. Then I played against him once when I was at Texas A&M and we could hardly stop him, even though we tied them in the game.

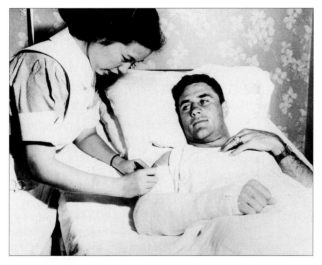

Recovering from an injury at the U.S. Open in Dallas in 1952, Doak observes as a nurse signs his cast.

"And a few years later, there we are in the (NFL) championship game and he's been hurt all year, and whoosh — there he goes for the big score. When he ran, he would just sort of glide down the field.

"I think the reason he was so hard to tackle is that he was really running harder and faster than you thought he was."

In 1953, the Lions added Harley Sewell, an all-American guard from the University of Texas — bringing the count of Texans on the Detroit squad to eight. Walker scored 93 points and led the team in receiving with 30 catches for 502 yards.

"Landing with the Lions was one of the best things that ever happened in my life," says Sewell, who played for Detroit for 10 years and has been a Rams scout since 1964. "And Doak is one of the finest people I ever met.

"He's always been the most unselfish, kind, good-hearted person — and that was especially noticeable to me then, because I was a rookie. But Doak treated everybody well, rookies included.

"He was also an amazing athlete who could play just about any position. There wasn't a game or sport that he couldn't pick up and get pretty good at within 30 or 40 minutes. I think he could have been a bull rider if he'd wanted, or anything else."

In the championship game, the halftime score was Walker 10, Cleveland 3 (he had scored a TD, kicked a field goal and an extra point) — but the Browns rallied to take a six-point lead late in the game.

But Layne then drove Detroit 80 yards in two minutes. With the ball at the Cleveland 33, he typically disregarded a call from the bench — a screen pass — and threw deep to Doran for the score. Walker added the PAT, and Cleveland was beaten again.

"That was pure Bobby," Lary says. "Most competitive guy I ever saw — the guy who said he wanted to run out of breath and money at the same time, and anything over (age) 39 was a bonus.

"That's the way he lived and that's the way he played. On the field, he was the leader and he called the game. Everybody tried to play like Bobby, but nobody ever could."

In 1954, the Lions won the West for the third year in a row, closing the regular season with a 14-10 cross-over win over Cleveland — bringing their record to 4-0 against the

Doak makes a desperate lunge for a Bobby Layne pass during a 56-10 loss to Cleveland in the 1954 NFL playoffs.

Browns in a three-year span.

But when they met again in the championship game a week later, it was a different story. Otto Graham produced six TD's (three rushing, three passing) and the Browns crushed the Lions, 56-10.

"That was a weird game," Walker says. "If you look at the statistics, they were pretty even. But everything we did was wrong, and everything they did was right."

But Sewell's recollection is that "Cleveland just whipped us real good — a lot of those Browns had a good day."

It has been suggested to Sewell that perhaps the Browns were simply tired of losing to Detroit.

"I dunno," he says. "I don't see how anyone could get that tired."

In 1955, the Lions seemed a little tired themselves — slumping to 3-9 in the middle of a run that otherwise carried them to seasons of 7-4-1, 11-3, 11-2, 9-3-1, 9-3 and 10-4 between 1951 and '57. There seemed to be a carryover from the shocking loss to the Browns, as Detroit opened with

six consecutive defeats and eventually lost five games by seven points or less.

The team recovered in 1956 — losing the conference championship on the final day of the season to Chicago, in the famous game in which Ed (Country) Meadows of the Bears broke Layne's jaw with a flagrantly illegal hit.

In 1957, the conference title was decided when Detroit and San Francisco met in a playoff at Kezar Stadium. With a commanding 24-7 halftime lead, the 49ers piled into their dressing room and began celebrating — somewhat prematurely.

"In that stadium, the team's locker rooms were adjacent to each other," Sewell says. "And they were, shall we say, inexpensively built.

"We sat there during the half and listened to every word they said."

In the second half, the Lions launched an incredible comeback and rolled over San Francisco's bon vivants, 31-27. Then, with Tobin Rote throwing for 280 yards and four touchdowns, they crushed the Browns, 59-14, to avenge the '54 loss.

But by that time, Walker was gone.

"I loved playing for the Lions," he says. "Buddy Parker was the perfect coach — we had assembled that team, and he kept it together and we had great success with it.

"One of the advantages to pro ball, of course, is that nobody graduates. You can keep a team together five or six years, and every year you know who's coming back.

"It was a fun time for me — the club had some great owners, and they let you know they cared about you. It was an era of loyalty, which I'm not sure you have now — but we almost became like a big family.

"The club would throw parties for us, and they'd give you a new TV set or something — just something to let you know we were all on the same team. Maybe it's a little hard to understand now, but it was just a different era.

"Football was good to me — the Lions were good to me. I traveled all over the world, and in every city we went to, you had friends there who would come see you. We won a lot, but we also had a lot of fun."

For Walker, part of the fun was being reunited with the rowdy, hard-drinking Layne, who in later life once reminded one and all that "if a man can't get his work done by noon, he shouldn't be working."

But in the 1950's, Layne worked hard enough to leave

"I loved playing for the Lions. Buddy Parker was the perfect coach — we had assembled that team, and he kept it together and we had great success with it.

Doak Walker

behind a trail that landed him in the Pro Football Hall of Fame.

"Playing with Bobby made it all a little easier," Walker says. "In a way, it was like playing at Highland Park. Bobby would drop back, look one way, then throw across the field to a spot where he knew I would be when the ball arrived. We'd been doing it since we were kids."

It was a magic time for the boys in the sky-blue shirts, a magic time for delirious fans in the Motor City, a magic time for a sport that would soon grow bigger and richer, and lose its personality.

It was four decades ago, and still they call each other on the phone, and fly halfway across the country for a reunion. The reunions are not held every five years, or every 20 years. They happen every summer, at Thurman McGraw's place in northern Colorado. Sometimes, there will be a ceremony in Detroit, and they all go back. Every time one of them is enshrined in the Hall of Fame, Canton is awash in Lions.

"There was a lot of camaraderie then," Sewell says. "I guess back then, we all played because we loved the game, and enjoyed being with each other. It sure wasn't because they paid us a whole lot.

"But in those days, you thought of it kind of like the family business. Everybody liked everybody, and you would never be traded ..."

In 1955, Doak Walker scored 106 points, played in his fourth Pro Bowl in six years, and made the highest income of his career — $35,000, because he got 40 percent of the gate from a game played in Dallas. Then he retired.

"Somebody offered me a better-paying job," he says.

So he left, having scored 534 points, accumulated more than 4,000 yards in tandem offense, and been named consensus All-Pro in four of his six years.

During the season, for the last time in his playing career, Walker was featured on the cover of yet another national magazine — *Sports Illustrated*. Two other *SI* covers that year featured a pair of Olympic skiers — brother and sister — named Buddy and Skeeter Werner.

More than a decade later, this would prove to be an ironic convergence.

CLOWNING LIONS: Doak and Detroit teammates (left to right) Jim Doran, Les Bingaman and Lou Cheekman at summer practice prior to the 1953 College All-Star Game.

After a Glorious Career, the Great Doaker Retires

Coming down out of Rabbit Ears Pass toward Steamboat Springs, Colorado, one is strongly tempted to find an amenable patch of ground and settle in.

It's what Doak Walker did, long ago.

"I loved football," he says. "I loved it when I was a little kid, I loved it when I was a young man playing it, and I didn't retire in 1955 because I had lost the desire.

"But I had achieved just about everything that I felt I could. I had been All-Pro, I had played on NFL championship teams, I had been treated well, paid well by the standards of the day, and accumulated a lifetime of memories. Football was good to me.

"But I always knew it was something you couldn't do forever, and I didn't want to be one of those guys who stayed a year too long. I didn't want to leave burned out, or crippled."

He stops for a moment, then grins.

"So, I got out with both my knees, all my teeth, and," shaking his head and crossing his eyes, "most of my faculties."

At age 28, he bid good-bye to a life that had always revolved around football and became a businessman.

"I went to work for the George A. Fuller Company, a national contractor in the construction business, and was originally based in Dallas," he says. "But in 1956, they transferred me to Denver."

A fateful and ironic transfer: the man many consider

CHAPTER ELEVEN

Born and bred a Texan, Doak found contentment in retirement in the Colorado mountains.

to be the greatest Texan ever to flash across the college football map has spent 41 of his 70 years as a resident of Colorado.

"I fell in love with Colorado when my father used to bring me up here to that camp as a kid," he says. "I've had a wonderful life up here, and I've never seen any reason to leave."

During the coming years, Walker became involved in several business ventures that were successful in varying degrees.

"I worked for a number of years basically as a business representative in the construction business," he says, "and it involved a lot of traveling. The first company I was with had offices all over the place. I was living in Boulder for a while and then they sent me to Cheyenne, then they decided to transfer me to Alaska.

"So I resigned and went back to Denver."

He went into business for a while with an old teammate, Cloyce Box, and also "had an interest in a couple

Doak married former Olympic skier Skeeter Werner in 1969. They met in 1966 while filming a TV skiing series.

of sporting goods stores in Dallas that did pretty well."

He worked his way up to the executive level with Fic-shbach & Moore, an electrical contractor, and eventually had his own company — Walker Chemicals — which he sold several years ago.

The son of a coach, he had some aspirations in that direction himself. Things never quite worked out — although Walker, Layne and Harley Sewell had great fun coaching the Texas squad to increasingly lopsided wins in the "Big 33" high school all-star games against Pennsylvania.

He was a backfield coach for one year with the Denver Broncos, but was among those swept aside when a new regime came in.

In 1967, he joined Tobin Rote as a coach with the Akron Vulcans of the Continental League — a short-lived

venture that came to an abrupt end when some gentlemen representing the interests of a loan organization arrived and carted off the gate receipts after a game.

In 1959, he was inducted into the College Football Hall of Fame — a short 10 years after his SMU career ended. Inducted with him were Army's Doc Blanchard and Georgia's Charlie Trippi — both of whom had played their last college game in 1946 — and the rest were old-timers.

Recognition for his achievements with the Lions took considerably longer. When he was finally inducted — along with Paul Hornung, Fran Tarkenton, Ken Houston and Willie Lanier — in 1986, he jokingly remarked how fitting it was that he had been nominated by the "Old Timers Committee."

It is the general figuring that the holdup was due to the

THE DOAKER RETIRES

Lifelong friend and teammate Bobby Layne presented Doak when he was inducted into the Pro Football Hall of Fame in 1986.

brevity — six seasons — of his career. But since he was All-Pro in four of them and played prominent roles in two NFL championship victories, the ground beneath him was pretty solid. Plus, he had actually played both ways in 1954 — one of the last NFL players to do so.

Once, in an interview, he had remarked that, "Games always came easy for me ... that can make things harder later, when things don't come as easy."

In 1965, after several years of gradually drifting apart, the two halves of the Walker family split. Doak stayed in Denver while Norma took the couple's four children — Laurie, Kris, Russell Doak and Scott, then aged 2 to 13 — and returned to Dallas.

After 15 years, the storybook marriage of the football hero and the beauty queen had ended.

The following year, Walker agreed to do a syndicated promotional shoot in New York in which he received six skiing lessons from an expert instructor. The six episodes aired nationally.

The instructor was Skeeter Werner — who had appeared on the *Sports Illustrated* cover in 1955 as she and her brother prepared for the '56 Winter Olympics in Cortina.

"At the time," she says, "I wasn't really sure who he was. I had heard of him, but actually, my brother and I had always been big Bobby Layne fans."

Over the next three years, however, a casual acquaintance grew finally into a whirlwind courtship.

Having bumped into each other a few times, they finally became seriously involved, Walker says, "When I came into Steamboat with another couple about midnight one night, and I ran into Skeeter's brother (Loris) in a bar. He suggested I call her, so I did — at 2 a.m.

"I picked her up at six the next morning and we went skiing. That night, we went to dinner — our first date — then took a sleeping bag to the foot of the mountain. The next morning, we got up, cooked bacon and eggs, then in the afternoon we played nine holes of golf and a set of tennis.

"The next day, her mother drove us over to Boulder, and I caught a plane for Detroit, where I had some business. We planned to meet in Palm Springs the next weekend to play golf.

"In the middle of the week, she called and said to meet her in Phoenix instead. She had some friends in Scottsdale, so we went to a couple of cocktail parties, took a swim, went to dinner at Trader Vic's, went back and sat on the diving board, and about 10:30 she says, 'I want to get married.'

"So we went to Las Vegas and got married."

A typical Walker routine ... the dizzy, whirlwind drive to win the game. Or in this case, the girl.

In the 28 years since, Walker has grown fond of saying, "Around here (Steamboat), I'm just Mr. Werner."

That is hardly the case, but the Werners of Steamboat Springs have indeed been a formidable sporting clan.

Sitting on land once wrested with great difficulty from the great Ute chief Ouray, Steamboat is now a charming community ranking with Vail and Aspen in the ski resort trade. From it, in the 1950's and 60's, spread an amazing fan of Olympic skiers — all from the same family.

The first was Skeeter, who competed in the world championships in Sweden in 1954 and was on the Olympic alpine team at Cortina in 1956.

Then came Buddy, who competed in the winter games in 1956, '60 and '64 and was the first American male skier to win a major European title — the Hannenkamm Downhill at Kitzbuhel, Austria, in 1959.

The youngest, Loris (Bugs) Werner, skied in the Winter Games at Innsbruck in 1964 and Grenoble in '68.

In the museum a block from the 82-year-old house

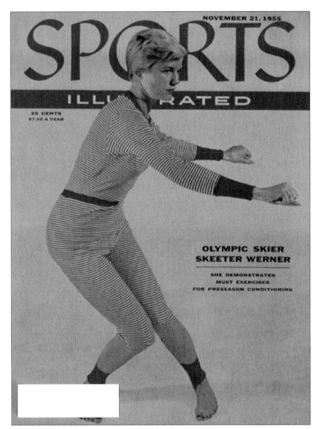

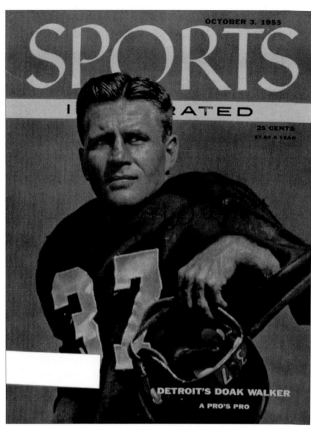

Doak and Skeeter graced the front covers of Sports Illustrated in Fall 1955.

where Doak and Skeeter live (the Werners bought it in 1941), there is a child's ski boot worn, in turn, by Skeeter, Buddy and Bugs.

In a glass case in the library a few blocks away are the opened pages of a book, *I Never Look Back* — the story of Buddy Werner, who was killed in an avalanche in Europe in 1964.

Outside the library is a large bronze of the family matriarch, Hazel, or "Hazy" — a woman of great kindness who died one night in a chair, reading a book.

There is also a great mountain looming over the town. It was once called Storm Mountain, but after Buddy's death it was renamed Mount Werner.

In Dallas, Norma Peterson Walker moved back into the familiar neighborhood around SMU, and set about raising her family. She remarried in 1968, and sent her children through Highland Park High School.

Following in certain footsteps, the sons, Russ and

Scott, became football stars.

But both say they were never pressured to emulate their famous father.

"Well, he certainly never pressured us," says Russ, who wound up playing three years as a defensive back at Colorado. "He never cared what we became — as long as it was what we wanted. He never tried to push us in any direction.

"About the only pressure I ever got was from people who kept reminding me to use my middle name on job applications, but I never did.

"We have never necessarily wanted to be what our father was — but we have always been proud of him."

That much is evident from various mementos in the spacious new home Russ and his wife, Lisa, have bought near the SMU campus.

There is a copy of the book written 47 years ago by Dorothy Kendall Bracken. There are laminated copies of the famous magazine covers from *Life*, *Sports Illustrated*, *Collier's* and *Look* — the latter two featuring Doak and Norma together. There is a copy of a book written by Ewell Sr., and a copy of the book on Buddy Werner, and the *SI* cover with Skeeter on it.

"I guess you could say there's just a lot of tradition in the family, and we're proud of all of it," says Scott, who at 33 is three years younger than his brother. "Also, it's something you never really get away from.

"When I was at the University of Texas, my dad came down for a father-son golf tournament — and all of the people there from his era were just awed. It was like the greatest celebrity of their lifetime was standing there, talking to them.

"Once, I met a guy who had dedicated an entire room of his house to my father. I couldn't believe it.

"But I guess it can be a little awe-inspiring for us, too ... when you can look at those magazine covers and it hits you: 'That's my mom and dad.' "

It has been a somewhat strange life for the four children — but one that seems to have turned out well.

"I think when my mom and dad split, it was harder on our sisters than it was on us," Scott says, "because they were older and had a greater adjustment to make."

Russ thinks so, too.

"Well, when we were a little older, we spent three months out of the year — all summer — up in Colorado with Dad," he says. "In a way, it was the best of both worlds. For us, it wasn't so terrible.

"Obviously, he wasn't here, and that was a problem. My mom raised all four of us. She taught us right from wrong, and saw to it that we grew up the way we should. All of the values we have, she instilled in us. Throughout our lives, she has been our mainstay.

"But my dad always kept up with what was going on, through his friends. I can remember him showing up at playoff games when I was at Highland Park, and the relationship that has developed over the years has been a good one.

"It's been an unusual situation, but I guess the main thing you could say about it is that we've always been proud of both our parents."

In any case, Scott says, the family legacy has always been there.

"I think we probably thought about it even as kids," he says. "When your parents are famous, everything you do is scrutinized a little more closely — and I think that one of the things that kept us out of trouble was that we didn't want to damage our family's name.

"Anyway, we seemed to have all turned out pretty well, and I think my dad is really proud of that."

Scott Walker is a marketing representative for Fults Management in Dallas; Russ is a partner in Solutions Unlimited, specializing in kitchen and bath products and accessories; Laurie is an interior space planner for several local firms; and Kris is raising three children in Highland Park.

For Walker, now 70, life has presented few insurmountable hurdles. It was once said of him that almost no one ever got a clear shot at him. It could perhaps also be said that the dark side of life never got a clear shot at him, either.

"Explain it?" he says, smiling. "I can't explain it. I don't know how it all happened. I was raised by wonderful people who gave me a set of values that have served me all my life.

"Other than that, I can only say that I was in exactly the right place at exactly the right time, I guess. What people chose to make of me, I had no control over."

True.

But it is nevertheless a fact that during his last three years at SMU, the school was forced by popular demand to move its operation into an arena three times the size of its original stadium.

And that he departed in 1949 as the only consensus three-time all-American in the history of the Southwest Conference — and in the 46 years of life that remained to that league, no one ever did it again.

And that although the SWC has crumbled into dust, Doak Walker will live — perhaps forever — in bronze. In a final act of deference — 35 years after he played his final game — the sculptor fixed the broken nose he had suffered in high school.

"I have led a blessed life," he says. "I don't know how anyone could be more blessed."

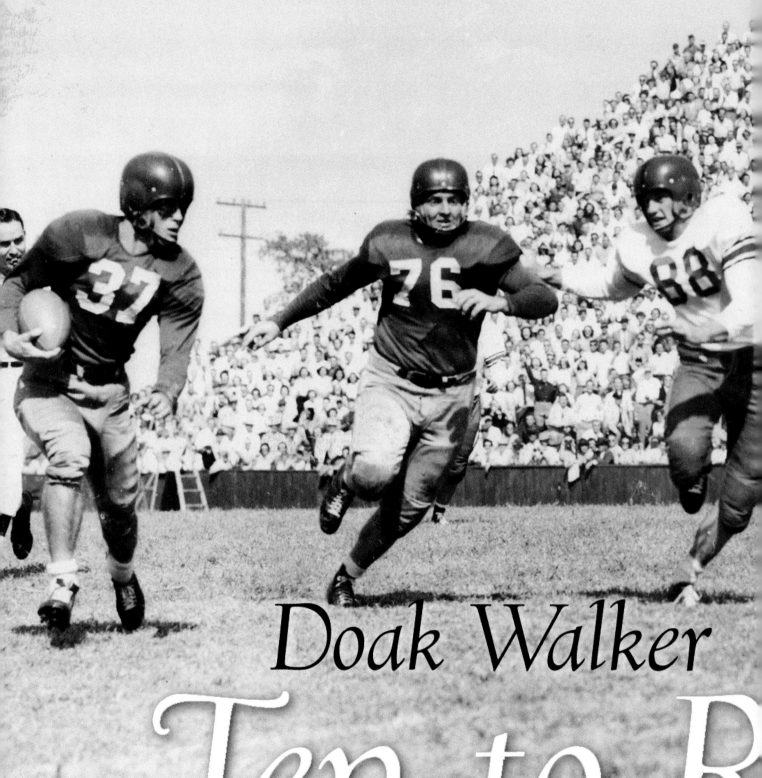

Doak Walker
Ten to R

emember

SMU Downs Broncos, 22-6

BY THE ASSOCIATED PRESS
Fort-Worth Star-Telegram

SAN FRANCISCO, Sept. 27, 1947

The Southern Methodist Mustangs, in a game filled with thrills, flying footballs and flashing runs, pounded out a 22-6 victory over Santa Clara on Saturday in San Francisco's Kezar Stadium.

Hero of the Methodist invasion was Doak Walker, the 175-pound Mustang quarterback from Dallas whose spectacular play drew resounding cheers from a partisan crowd of 5,000.

Late in the fourth quarter, Walker took a kickoff from Ellery Williams on his 3-yard line and raced the length of the field to a touchdown.

In the second quarter, Walker scored SMU's first touchdown from the 6-inch line on a play through center. The Mustangs fought their way up to the Bronco goal from their 39-yard line.

Two spectacular plays on the part of SMU paved the way to the goal line. On the first, Paul Page, SMU's halfback, fad-ed back from the Santa Clara 40-yard line, racing with his arm outstretched as if to pass. With the entire Santa Clara team out of position, he streaked to the other side of the field to be hauled down by the Santa Clara safety on the 35.

Walker repeated the trick from the opposite end of the field to set up the score.

Midway in the third quarter, Walker twice reversed the field and ran untouched from the Santa Clara 44. He converted the extra point on this play and his 97-yard

Doak visits with the press by telephone during SMU's visit to California.

touchdown, but missed the first one.

Walker accounted for all but two of the Methodists' points on the scoreboard.

Those two points came on a safety in the third quarter, when a Santa Clara lateral traveled too far backward and landed in the end zone.

Santa Clara, brilliant in the first quarter but listless after that, regained its fire in the fourth quarter, starting from deep in its territory and smashing all the way to the SMU goal against a Mustang second team.

Fullback William Prentice ripped off several long gains, one for 40 yards, to bring the Broncos within striking distance. Ben Sheridan passed to Donald Keck, Santa Clara's end, to place the ball on the SMU 9.

The Bronco touchdown occurred two plays later via a short pass to Keck over the goal line.

SCORE BY PERIODS

SMU	0	6	9	7	—	22
Santa Clara	0	0	0	6	—	6

Walker Sparks Ponies' 35-19 Win

BY FELIX R. MCKNIGHT
Fort-Worth Star-Telegram

DALLAS, Oct. 4, 1947

Magnificent Doak Walker was the blue-ribbon exhibit on State Fair's opening night, running like an unbroken stallion to bring an impressive Southern Methodist a 35-19 victory over Missouri in an offensive classic.

Walker, the shy sophomore candidate for All-America recognition, had everything at the right moments to first send his Mustangs into the lead and then haul them out of danger in the closing minutes.

Not one of the 26,000 perspiring Cotton Bowl fans would leave before the last wild play as the Missourians, masters of quick and powerful darts off the T-formation, breathed down the Mustangs' necks until the final few minutes.

In the final analysis, Walker, a 20-year-old former Highland Park hero back in the Mustang saddle after army service, was just about the ballgame with his crackling runs of 76 and 57 yards, his improved needle-eye passing and crafty signal calling.

The statistics almost prove that, Missouri, as fine an offensive club as has roamed these parts in several seasons, outgained the Methodists by ground and air, rolling up 306 yards to the SMU 301.

GAME 2 SMU VS. MISSOURI, 1947

The 1947 Mustangs won 9 games, tied 2, and were named Southwest Conference champions.

But they just didn't have a rocket to let loose and the Mustangs did — the man, Walker.

It could have been a different ballgame had not Walker pulled his slyest trick of magic midway through the fourth quarter.

The comfortable Methodist lead of 21-7 he had helped build with a 76-yard sideline dash, a smash through the line from the 2 after brilliantly leading a 63-yard drive and a 16-yard scoring pass to Howard Parker, suddenly had melted before a furious Missouri comeback.

The score was 21-19, with Don Faurot's Tigers getting wilder by the minute when Walker took off from his own 23-yard line behind a battered and weary line on what appeared to be an innocent gain of a couple of yards at right end. But suddenly he stopped, pivoted and drew out of a trap.

Like a lightning shaft, he cut to his left in the Missouri secondary and started one of the most brilliant runs the old Cotton Bowl has seen. He reached midfield amid a swarm of Missourians, cut straight across the 50-yard line for about 30 yards and then made his move down the sideline.

The Missouri passe raced at his heels - and he was out there alone with no blockers around. Finally, fleet Loyd Brinkman elbowed him out of bounds on the Missouri 20.

But it was the ballgame. Dick McKissack, the sparkling SMU fullback who had moments as great as Walker's, chipped in and helped Walker push to the 4.

There, Walker, limping from an aggravated heel injury, started a line plunge, drew up short and held the ball in back of him while Ed Green sneaked around from the wing-back post, stole it from his hands and almost jogged unnoticed deep around his left end for a touchdown on the famous Methodist trick play.

Of course, substitute back Gilbert Johnson came in and heaved a prodigious touchdown pass to Ed Green a few minutes later for the final score, but it was Walker who escaped from a Missouri ambush and the 57 yards he gained won the ballgame.

Three fine Missouri backs, Harold Entsminger, a picture player handling all the T-formation work; Ed Quirk, the bulldozer, 283-pound fullback who understandably holds the Big Six shot-put record; and Nick Carras had entirely changed the complexion of the game just a few minutes before.

Trailing, 21-7, the Tigers came out intent on making it a contest in six swirling minutes. It all started when Carras took an end-zone kickoff after the third Methodist score and scrambled to the 28, Entsminger started his vicious handoff plays to Quirk, Carras and Dick Braznell, another sparkler, and they rolled like a flood downfield to the SMU 11 against a positively befuddled SMU second string.

Then Braznell, a nifty left-handed passer, hit Fred Hulse with an end-zone touchdown pass. Bill Day, quite a kicker all evening, had his try blocked. It was 21-13.

It was obvious that Missouri was rolling, but the Methodist reserves stayed in for the next kickoff and quickly got SMU into a hole when Louis Burress' kick was partially blocked and recovered on the SMU 37.

The Methodist regulars tumbled back into the game, but they couldn't stop the Tigers' prairie fire. Braznell burrowed through the middle for 16 yards and after considerable nudging by Carras and Quirk in small chunks, Braznell breezed through on a quick opener for a score from the 3. Again, Day's kick was partially blocked and it was 21-19.

It was fireworks all the way, both teams sparring dangerously in the first quarter and SMU finally scoring first two minutes after the second quarter opened.

Walker bolted over from the Missouri 2 for the first score to climax a 63-yard drive he personally led.

Green started the drive from the SMU 37 with 6 yards on a handoff from Walker and then Bobby Folsom, receiving end back in Mustang harness after a wartime stint with the powerful Army team, gathered in a Walker heave just a step from the sideline for a first down at the Missouri 42.

The next six plays were served by Walker a la carte. He bolted through the middle for 16 on a beautifully delayed buck, crept stealthily around his right end for 13 more to the Missouri 9 and then, in successive jolts at the Tiger wall, finally got it across.

Naturally, it was Walker who added the extra point.

But Missouri came back with hurricane force to tie the score in short order.

Entsminger, the 181-pound T-man who was poison all night, fashioned a quick touchdown from the SMU 20 after Frank Payne, Walker's tailback replacement for the moment, fumbled on a pass attempt on second-and-1. It is normally a smart football play, but just in the wrong territory, and tackle Chester Fritz recovered for Missouri on the Mustang 20.

Entsminger handed off to Bob Hopkins and the fleet digger swept through a bewildered Methodist line to the 7. Entsminger added 2 more and then turned over the scoring chore to Quirk. Day added the extra-point kick.

A cleverly planned punt return gave Walker a chance to blow into the open a few minutes later and push SMU into a 14-7 halftime lead.

Brinkman booted far down to Ed Green on the SMU 20. He hesitated a split second, waited for Walker to swing around from the other side of the field and take a handoff on the SMU 24. Walker seemed to almost dance in one spot as he waited for blockers Brownie Lewis, Joe Etheridge and Earl Cook to clear the timber away.

Then, just a couple of feet from the sideline, he made his move and came tearing into the open and simply outran Missourians for the next 76 yards to the goal line. He was breathing hard — but he kicked the extra point.

It was just that kind of a game all the way. Something like Missouri gave Texas in the Cotton Bowl a couple of years ago.

SCORE BY PERIODS

Missouri	0	7	6	6	— 19
SMU	0	14	7	14	— 35

GAME 3 SMU VS. TEXAS, 1947

Unbeaten Ponies Spill Longhorns

BY FLEM HALL

Fort-Worth Star-Telegram

DALLAS, Nov. 1, 1947

What has been called a hooligan offense, which features a sucker play known as "the flicker," combined with a bewildering defense here at the Cotton Bowl this gray and blustery Saturday afternoon to bring Southern Methodist University a thin, but dazzling 14-13 victory over a University of Texas football team which appeared to have lost the edge from its razor-sharp early season form.

With Doak Walker and the wingbacks playing here, there and just about anywhere in the complicated offensive system fashioned by assistant coach H.H. (Rusty) Russell (the old high school master at Masonic Home and Highland Park), the Mustangs romped and passed for 211 yards against the sturdy Steer defenses to earn both scores.

The shifting and revolving defenses fashioned by SMU head coach Matty Bell slowed the Texas attack sufficiently to bring the ultimate decision to a matter of a conversion point.

The one-point difference in the score which just about reflected the difference between the teams for the tumultuous day, resulted from the failure of Frank Guess to convert after the second Texas touchdown. The place-kick, poorly hit, veered a little to the east of the north

Doak turns the corner against a stubborn Texas defense led by Max Bumgardner (81) and Tom Landry (24).

goal and the ball was deflected by a heavy quartering head wind.

Guess, a junior who otherwise had a brilliant day with a punting average of 51.8 yards, had booted the point after

the first Texas score.

If Guess was responsible for his team not getting a tie (a debatable point), Walker certainly won it for SMU. He kicked both extra points for the Ponies, besides doing just

126

Doak hurdles through the middle of the Longhorns' line. He eventually scored a TD and both extra points.

1947
SMU...14
TEXAS..13

Laughead

Walker(37) takes Johnsons' pass on 18 and goes to 4 yard line to set up second touchdown. Page(18) blocked Texas(24)

about everything else.

Walker, a 168-pound sophomore all-position back overshadowed every other player on the field, and there were a great many exceptionally able pigskin rustlers on the emerald green sod during the two hours of furious conflict.

But this is a story of team play. There were individual feats and duels that cut like flares thought the play, but that is another story.

The malevolent Mustangs were never behind in the swirling battle. They led 7-0; were tied 7-7, led 14-7 and 14-13.

SMU went 19 and 74 yards for its touchdowns. Texas sailed 32 and 71 for its scores.

The Mustangs needed six plays for the 19-yard dash in the first 3:06 of play. Only five plays, though, were needed on the 74-yard jaunt in the second quarter.

The Longhorns lunged the 32 yards on eight plays in the early minutes of the second quarter to tie the score

at 7. Nine plays were required on the 71-yard move that started in the third quarter and carried over into the final period.

In retrospect, it might look different, but at this excited moment in the wild and washing wake of the scrimmage that tore up the grass roots before 45,700 witnesses, it seems inevitable that the spindle-shanked Horses, who were fired to a high degree, and the lean and lethal Longhorns have provided the substance for another bright chapter in the saga of football at its best.

It can't be said with any justification that there was any real difference between the teams. In reviewing the constantly recurring peaks of play, there were times when a half step here, a split-second there would have reversed the decision.

Texas actually gained a mite more yardage from scrimmage (226-211) but they lost a few more to end up with a net of 197 to SMU's 199.

It was that close.

Texas was still in the ballgame after what proved to be the final score was emblazoned on the scoreboard.

Midway through the fourth quarter, the Steers had the ball on the SMU 32 with second-and-1 for first down. Jim Canady slanted through the line for 16 yards, but the Texas left tackle had been offside. Instead of being first down on the 16, it was second-and-6 on the 37. Tommy Landry failed to gain, but Bob Layne passed to Byron Gillory for 4 yards.

Then came the play that sealed the fate of the team which had slugged the previous rivals into decisive defeat.

SMU, the team which had previously pressed past five major opponents, rose to the challenge.

With fourth-and-2, quarterback Layne gambled, as he should have, with only six minutes to play. He tried for the first down with a running play — with the Lancing Landry hitting his left guard.

It might have worked, but in his driving eagerness, Landry's foot slipped. He didn't fall, but he did not get the power he needed. He stumbled weakly into the waiting arms of John Hambergers and Cecil Sutphin, who stopped him in his tracks short of the first down.

SMU took the ball and everyone in the stadium knew the game was over.

There is no assurance, of course, that Texas would have made the first down, much less the touchdown, had there been no slip of the Landry foot, but it is sure that the slip did kill the Longhorns' last chance of escaping defeat.

It is entirely possible that SMU won the game with the first play of the game — an 81-yard runback of the kickoff that knocked the poised and confident Steers loose from their moorings.

Frank Payne, a last-minute starter, took Guess' boot deep in the end zone; ran out to the 8 and then handed off to Paul Page, who swung far and fast to the west sideline as he cut toward the north goal.

It was a planned play. The SMU blockers cut the Orange tacklers down and formed what looked like a puncture-proof convoy around the ball carrier. Only great work by Billy Pyle and the speed of his teammates hauled Page down on the 19.

The next three plays netted nothing, but on fourth down the imperturbable Walker took his time and coldly passed to Dick McKissack for a first down on the Texas 4.

McKissack pulled the defense in with a plunge into the middle that made 2 yards. On the next play, Walker called the belittled flicker — a play the Longhorns had been warned about.

Walked took the snap back and hit into the line, but as he hit, Page racing from the right-wing post, took the ball at Walker's hip and swung around Dale Schwartzkopf and Canady for the touchdown.

A 10-yard return by Gillory started the Steers to their first touchdown — the 32-yard move that started in the first quarter and paid off in the second.

Layne passed to Schwartzkopf for 8 yards and later, on fourth down, to Max Bumgardner for 11 yards and a first down on the 13. From there, the Longhorns rammed it across on pure power, with Landry doing most of the work to tie the game at 7.

SMU came again. Page returned a punt 24 yards to his 26. McKissack made 3. Gilbert Johnson was substituted into the backfield and Walker moved into the blocking-back hole. On a handoff, he passed to Sid Halliday for 10. McKissack hit again for 5.

Then came the payoff. Johnson took the snap at tailback, waited and then spiraled a shot deep and slightly to the right. Walker made a magnificent catch on the 25 and raced Gillory toward the flag in the southwest corner.

With a superman effort, Gillory knocked Doak out on the 2-yard line, but it was no use. On the first play, McKissack bulled over and Walker converted.

It made no difference that Layne was able later to pass 14 yards to Gillory for a touchdown — because Guess missed the extra point.

SCORE BY PERIODS

Texas	0	7	0	6	— 13
SMU	7	7	0	0	— 14

SMU Whip Hogs, 14-6, In Wild Game

BY FLEM HALL

Fort-Worth Star-Telegram

DALLAS, Nov. 15, 1947

fired-up herd of University of Arkansas Razorbacks lost, 14-6, to a favored Southern Methodist University's Mustangs Saturday afternoon in a terrific football game that saw everything on the rough side, including two attacks on officials.

If it hadn't been for the rules and the willingness of the officials to call them, the Razorbacks, last year's co-champions, might have knocked off the undefeated and untied Mustangs. But as it was, SMU came from behind to win with something to spare.

During the game, a man who appeared to be the Arkansas trainer shoved field judge Charley Hawn when the latter stepped over the sideline in front of the Arkansas bench to mark the spot where a Porker receiver had stepped out of bounds.

Immediately after the game, a fan rushed out of the stands and onto the field and piled into referee Jack Sisco, who promptly knocked the attacker down with a flurry of blows. Sisco attempted to press his counterattack, but was pulled off by other officials. No one else

participated in the melee.

A total of 16 penalties were called in the game and officials stepped off 126 yards (nine for 81 yards against Arkansas and seven for 45 against the Mustangs). But the Razorbacks were repeatedly damaged severely by penalties that occurred at critical moments.

The attack on Sisco was unprovoked. As a matter of fact, he called relatively few of the penalties.

Arkansas drove 27 yards on four plays in the first quarter to take a 6-0 lead, Leon (Muscles) Campbell made the final 15 with a bull charge through the middle.

SMU, with the aid of one drive-sustaining penalty, moved 81 yards on 14 plays in the second quarter and went ahead, 7-6, when Doak Walker's conversion kick was good.

There was no scoring in the third quarter as SMU kept command of the situation, but the Ponies pushed 31 yards on seven plays and one penalty in the fourth and again Walker converted to seal the victory.

The game, though, was rough from the start and most of the costly calls were on fouls which were clearly seen from away the press box.

The sideline shoving occurred in the fourth quarter when the score was 7-6. Clyde Scott passed down the east sideline to Billy Bass.

Bass made the catch at the SMU 40, stepped along the sideline for a few paces and then broke loose to go to the SMU 5 where he lost the ball to SMU on a fumble that resulted from a tackle. As Bass ran, Hawn marked a spot where he thought Bass had stepped off the field. Occupants of the Arkansas bench protested vigorously and a man who was said to be the team trainer shoved Hawn.

Doak and his coach, Matty Bell, savor their glorious 1947 season.

Fuel was added to the fire, when the entire play was called back by umpire Rosco Minton, who called offensive shoving against the Razorbacks. That moved the Razorbacks to their own 30-yard line and set up the situation that led to SMU's second touchdown.

Scott fumbled and Dick McKissack recovered on the Arkansas 31.

Three plays made 6 yards and SMU was penalized 5 back to the 30. Disdaining to punt on fourth down, Walker ran wide to the right. It appeared that he was trapped for a big loss, but he reverse his field to the left, picked up blockers and raced for a 16-yard gain and a first down on the Arkansas 14.

McKissack picked up 2 yards and caught a Walker pass for a first down on the 2-yard line. From there, Walker sliced over for the score.

It was the sad misfortune of the visitors from the

Ozarks to be called for defensive holding in the second quarter when they had stopped what later proved to be the 81-yard scoring drive. On fourth-and-3 on their 25, the Mustangs punted, but the holding penalty canceled the play and gave SMU a first down.

The Mustangs needed no more help. With Gilbert Johnson passing and Page, Walker and McKissack carrying, the red and blue delighted the capacity homecoming crowd of 23,000 by rolling relentlessly down the field, into the teeth of the wind for a score.

Walker's conversion really won the game. Just as it did two weeks ago when his placekicks gave SMU a 14-13 edge over Texas.

SCORE BY PERIODS

SMU	0	7	0	7	— 14
Arkansas	6	0	0	0	— 6

Inspired Frogs Tie SMU, 19-19

By Amos melton
Fort-Worth Star-Telegram

FORT WORTH, Nov. 29, 1947

P sychiatrists and steam shovel operators are going to have a big Christmas in these parts. By conservative estimates, the boys with the big scoops have a steady job for weeks shoveling the fingernails out of TCU Stadium.

As for the medics who take care of nervous breakdowns — they can just get their soft couches and dim lights all ready for 32,000 limp and babbling individuals who will be dropping around at any time.

The wacky folks will be the unfortunates — or fortunates — who sat on the slope of Frog Field on Saturday afternoon and saw TCU and SMU dash and drive to a 19-19 tie in their traditional game.

Without a single dissenting vote, the duel was voted the most hilarious, drama-dipped and nerve-shattering in the history of the long series. So throat-clutching were the goings-on, that most folks won't be able to swallow until Monday.

With the kind assistance of a soda water boy (he's

holding the still-quivering typewriter steady) here's a hazy account of what happened.

The Frogs, sharp and ready, roared to a 12-0 lead in the first 17 minutes. The Ponies, led by Doak Walker, who played one of the greatest games in conference history, came back strong, kept nibbling at the lead and finally shoved ahead late in the third, 13-12.

That brought things up to the last two minutes and those final 120 seconds were as wild as any in the memory of any living football fanatic. Everything happened.

The ever-battling Christians, operating from behind their 10-yard line, went exactly 80 yards on two plays!

Yep, that's correct. The mighty little Lindy Berry

132

Walker out distances Frogs as he rambles 76 yards for score.

hurled a pass and lanky Morris Bailey, a sophomore end, reached up for a great catch at about the Frog 40.

Ponies were all about but Morris spun free, took off in an open field and seemed gone. Then, as Walker and Paul Page began to converge on him about the Frog 20, Morris cut across the field and spied Charley Jackson coming up fast.

Just as he was tackled, Bailey flipped a backward pass that traveled 15 yards square into Jackson's eager hands and the halfback broke for the east sideline.

But he was finally collared on the Pony 8-yard line.

On first down, Berry called a single wing and started what looked like a straight off-tackle play. But just as he was hit at about the 5, the little man whirled and flipped a lateral out to big Pete Stout, who had floated wide.

It was a low toss, but Stout scooped up the potato and there wasn't anything but daylight to six-point territory. He made it in a leap. Berry, the darling of the Frog fans, was hurt on the magnificent effort and received an echoing ovation as he left the field.

Then Wayne Pitcock kicked the extra point to make

TEXAS COLLEGE FOOTBALL LEGEND **DOAK WALKER**

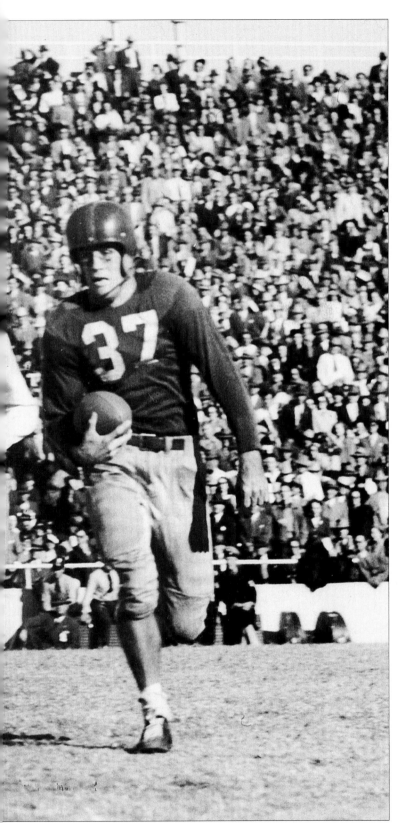

it 19-13, and the 32,000 fans were sure the Frogs had won because there was only 1:40 to play.

But they reckoned without darting Doak. Walker wasn't gonna take a licking. He took the kickoff, faked a handoff and then shot up the east sideline in a white-shirted blur.

The Frogs converged valiantly but were blocked or just missed tackles. Walker broke into the open spaces and seemed gone, but the Frogs' Randy Roger had held back as the safety man and he finally shoved Walker over the sideline on the Frog 36.

Matty Bell rushed Gilbert Johnson, his ace hurler, to the mound but his first two efforts were high. Then Walker got in the act again. He sneaked out, made a fine jumping snatch of Johnson's pass on the Frog 15, and was dropped on the 10. There were 20 seconds to play.

While the ushers rushed to the aid of fainting old ladies and swooning co-eds, Johnson started a run as if to sweep the Frog left end. Then he planted his feet and passed.

It was a rifle shot of some 12 yards that plugged end Sid Halliday right on the goal line.

Halliday was hit hard by two Frogs as the ball arrived but he held to the precious leather like a mama kangaroo pocketing a youngun. It was a score that made it 19-19.

Then, in a mighty hush — while the 32,000 hardly dared breathe — Doak made his try for the all-important point. It was wide to the left and as referee Jack Sisco brushed the grass with his no-good sign, the throng roared with the thunder of a 105mm barrage.

That ended it. Carl Knox, playing his last second for the Frogs, tried mightily to return the kickoff for another score but he was dropped on the Frog 14, and the tremendous game ended before another play.

Thus, the Frogs put the only blemish on SMU's record for the season and prevented then from earning their second perfect year in history.

And no one could say either side was lucky. They deserved just that — a tie. The Ponies had an edge in the statistics, but in a way they were fortunate to count again

Doak, who had one of his finest games at SMU, rambles around end for big yardage against the Horned Frogs.

in so little time.

One thing is sure, the Ponies had it when they had to have it. Or rather, you could say Walker had it. He was the difference all afternoon.

So both teams go to bowls — SMU to the Cotton and TCU to the Delta. If it were possible, the best game might be a rematch of the old rivals. Surely, few in this sector were as good as this one. Even veteran writers thought it was more exciting than that legendary 1935 duel between undefeated teams. This one was a honey.

The deadlock gives SMU a clear title with only a tie, while the Frogs won fourth place.

From the outset, it was evident that the Frogs were ready. After five minutes of play, they blasted 50 yards on seven plays for the first score. Bailey and Stout were the heroes. Morris made his first terrific catch for a first down on the Pony 13.

From there, the bull rush of Stout scored in just four plays. He blasted two steps for the counter. Pitcock missed the extra point.

Walker almost scored on the ensuing kickoff (the guy was dynamite all day), but was stopped on the Frog 23, after 77 yards. But the threat died on the Frog 4.

On the last play of the first quarter, Johnson's pass bounced off Walker's shoulder and the Frogs' Orien Browning intercepted in a flash and broke into the open, picking up great blocking.

He was forced finally to cut back on the 12, and was dropped on the SMU 8 after a 56-yard gain.

Berry made it to the 2 on three tries and on fourth down, the ever-ready Stout just went over the top at the middle for his second touchdown. This time, Pitcock's point try was blocked. The crowd could hardly believe what it had seen.

The Mustangs then settled to their chores. Just before the half, they were messing around on their 38, where it was second-and-11. Mr. Walker dropped back to pass, wasn't rushed too fast, and took off around the Frog left end.

He turned the corner at the sideline, paced himself for blockers about the Frog 40, then soared into the open and went 61 yards for SMU's first tally.

Walker missed the extra point.

The Frogs probably will be kicking themselves in their old age for missing two fine opportunities early in the third. Randy Rogers recovered a fumble by Dick McKissack on the Pony 17, but the chance died with Page intercepting Berry's pass in the end zone on fourth down.

Two Mustang plays later, a low pass-back skidded between Walker and McKissack and the Frogs' Wayne Rogers bounced on the leather only 5 yards from the Pony goal. But even this great opportunity died when three runs and a pass failed. Walker knocked down the pass to Jackson, just when it seemed Jackson had held it in the end zone for another tally.

SMU took the lead just as the third ended. The Ponies went 31 yards on 13 plays, the most damaging being passes from Walker to hooking ends.

From the 3-yard line on second down, Walker raced wide to his right and as David Bloxoym missed a tackle on the 5-yard line, went over in the corner. rambles also added the extra point to put SMU ahead, 13-12 — which is where the real excitement began.

There isn't room here to adequately praise the fine players on either side. But, you would have to start with Walker.

Dick Reinking, Raleigh Blakely, Lloyd Baxter, Joe Etheridge, Floyd Lewis and a half-dozen others did their share.

For the Frogs, loudest praise must go to Stout, who scored three times; Bailey, who was simply great; George Boal; Wayne and Randy Rogers; Dave Bloxom; Scratch Edwards; and Harold Kilman, who was, perhaps, the best lineman on the field.

And you can't forget young Dick Lowe, the freshman who was the only right guard left on offense after Bull Hicks was hurt. Lowe earned his letter in a big way Saturday.

SCORE BY PERIODS

SMU	0	6	7	6	— 19
TCU	6	6	0	7	— 19

Bell, Meyer Spread Praise

By Lorin McMullen
Fort Worth Star-Telegram

The gun sounded, ending a tremendous game at a peak of excitement after Texas Christian University had stormed 80 yards to seize a 19-13 lead only to watch Southern Methodist sweep the length of the field, get a 19-19 tie and then miss the extra point.

Matty Bell, the Mustangs' head coach, strode directly to midfield to shake hands with his life-long friend, L.R. (Dutch) Meyer, chief of the Frog staff.

"Congratulations, Dutch," he said, "that one ought to bring them back, huh? Seriously, you sent a fine team against us, you deserved to win."

Meyers, equally friendly, told Bell he had a great team and wished him good luck.

Bell, with his assistant coaches, moved on to the Mustang dressing room, where he seemed disappointed as he went through the motions of patting on the back his players.

Suddenly, Matty broke into a big smile.

"Say," he exclaimed, "I feel fine! Why, we're the conference champions! We don't have to share any title with (University of) Texas! There you are, Doak. You're the champs! Everything's fine boys!"

Later, Bell gave more credit to TCU and its players. It was a hard-fighting team, an alert team, a hard team to beat, he said.

Doak Walker, who had one of the greatest days of his career, was lavish in his praise of the Frogs.

Exhausted, still nervous and breathing hard, the little Mustang wizard carefully weighed his words:

"What a gallant effort that was by the TCU line!" he said. "Believe me it was tough from end to end. It really gave us a working over. Anyone in particular? Well, I saw plenty of that big Weldon (Scratch) Edwards. Another fellow I thought played a terrific game was fullback Pete Stout. Was he ever hard to hold!"

Walker declined to compare TCU with Texas or some of the other teams which extended SMU.

"Well, no other team tied us this year and I'll say that TCU deserved everything it go today,"he said.

Doak said his try for extra point in the last second or two of play missed the goal posts, exactly as the official called it. The ball carried about a foot to the left, he said.

Over in the Frog dressing room, Stout, who made all three Frog touchdowns, returned the compliments. He spoke of Walker as a "wizard" and then proclaimed, "but say, they told me SMU was composed of Walker and 10 unidentified men. Believe me, that isn't so!"

"Those other guys play football hard, too," Stout said. "Be more specific? Well, that fullback Dick McKissack, for one. Say, he's great."

Meyer's emotions were mixed with joy over the tie and regret that "we couldn't stop 'em in the clutch."

"But wasn't it a great game?" he said. "I thought it was one of the best I ever saw. Walker? Sure, he's a great football player, great competitor. Our star? Well, all of them. Tackle Harold Kilman played the greatest game of his career. And say he's the best tackle in the league."

Line coach Clyde Flowers also praised George Brown's defensive work and the contribution of Dick Lowe, the Wichita Falls freshman who filled in after Alan Pike went out after the Rice game and Morelle (Bull) Hicks was hurt early in the Mustang tilt.

That left only one right guard who could operate on offense — Lowe. He could and did.

Davey O'Brien, TCU's All-American in 1938, saw the game and said he was "really proud of the Frogs."

About Walker, he said: "Doak's tops, a truly great player and a great team man. He's about the best in the business at setting things up for his blockers. There's no one better anywhere at maneuvering."

Walker & Rote Lead Mustangs

By The Associated Press
Fort-Worth Star-Telegram

PITTSBURGH, Sept. 25, 1948

The Mustangs of Southern Methodist University trampled Pittsburgh, 33-14, Saturday on solid running by star Doak Walker and sharp passing by Gilbert Johnson.

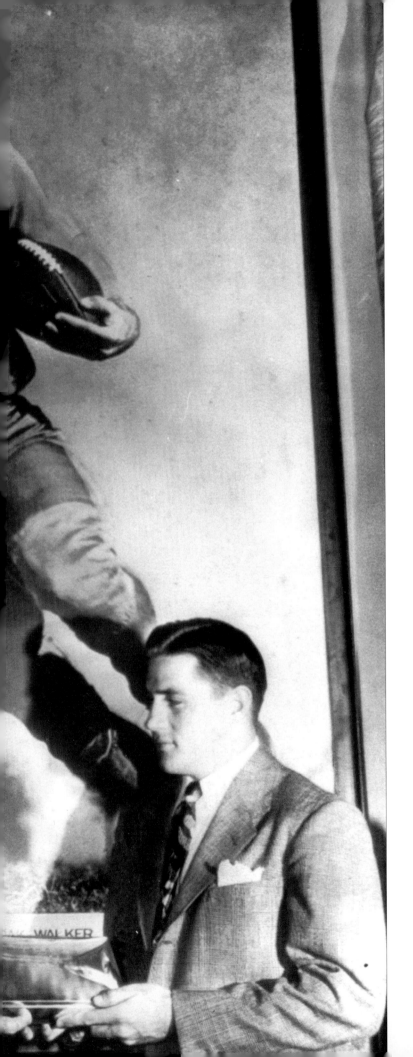

Pitt pushed across two touchdowns on passes into the end zone in the final quarter. SMU's Johnson rivaled Walker as the star performer. He threw nine passes, all completed, and accounted for a gain of 207 yards.

Walker, the man the crowd of 31,400 wanted most to see, completed 3 of 4 passes for 33 yards. He pitched one for SMU's first touchdown. Walker also caught a touchdown pass and ran 76 yards for a third score on a punt return.

SMU scored at the end of the first quarter when Walker threw a 13-yard pass to Raleigh Blakely in the end zone.

The next SMU score occurred in the second quarter, with Johnson standing on his 40 and tossing to Walker, who ran from the Pitt 30 to the goal line.

The half ended with SMU leading, 14-0.

In the third quarter, Walker caught a Pitt punt on his 26 and tore across the goal line without being touched.

A SMU fumble led to a Pitt touchdown in the fourth quarter. After the bobble, Cecconi threw a pass from the SMU 20 to Bill Bruno in the end zone.

SMU then got two touchdowns, one on Johnson's 40-yard pass to Blakely and one on Johnson's pass to Kyle Rote.

Rote caught that pass on the Pitt 41, evaded one tackler and ran for a score.

In the final two minutes, Pitt got its second tally on Bob Lee's 13-yard pass to end Bill McPeak in the end zone.

SCORE BY PERIODS

SMU	7	7	6	13	—	33
Pitt	0	0	0	14	—	14

Doak, who won The Maxwell Award in 1947, began the 1948 season by scoring three TD's against Pitt.

Walker, Ponies Lasso Longhorns

BY FLEM HALL

Fort-Worth Star-Telegram

....

AUSTIN, TEXAS, Oct. 30, 1948

You've probably heard that Southern Methodist University defeated Texas, 21-6, at Memorial Stadium before 68,750 here this warm and windy autumn afternoon, but have you heard that the football game was a lot closer than the score? It was!

It's dangerous, in a controversial sort of way, to go back of the final figures on the scoreboard and say this or that almost came off, but the University of Texas Longhorns could, with just a little luck, have defeated the defending Southwest Conference champions from Southern Methodist University — the 15-point difference in the score notwithstanding.

We are not saying that SMU didn't have the better team or that the Crimson-helmeted Mustangs didn't deserve to win.

As the game was played, SMU did have the better team, and they did deserve to win. But the score should have been closer and Texas could have won.

They play off of the score and not the statistics, so we don't do more than refer you to the first downs (23-13) and yards gained (393 to 284), both in favor of Texas, and go on to other things — Doak Walker, for instance.

The dazzling Doak was a positive factor — a double-dyed all-American again.

He personally scored two of SMU's three touchdowns (one on a 67-yard run in the second minute of play), threw the pass that started the other touchdown, converted three times, carried nine times for 72 yards, completed both passes he attempted for 39 yards, caught three passes for 20 yards, punted four times for a 46-yard average, selected plays flawlessly, blocked well and made no mistakes of any kind, during about 55 minutes of double-duty services, that could be spotted from the press box.

Doak shows off SMU mascot, Peruna, to a pair of Mustang fans.

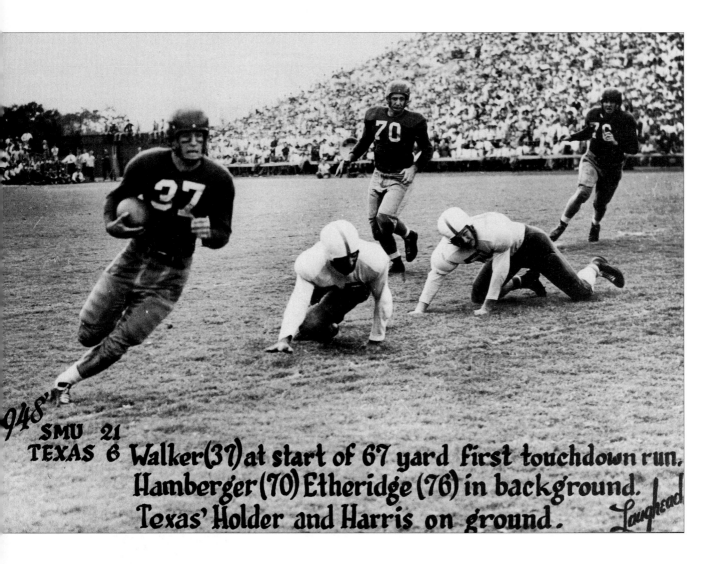

1948
SMU 21
TEXAS 6 Walker(37) at start of 67 yard first touchdown run.
Hamberger (70) Etheridge (76) in background.
Texas' Holder and Harris on ground.

He played four positions in the bewildering assortment of offensive formations employed by Coach Matty Bell.

Walker chilled and all but killed the Steers on the third play after the opening kickoff. This is the way it happened:

With third-and-7 on his 33, the 165-pound junior dropped back to pass, found no receiver, evaded three rushers, started slowly to his right, stepped on the gas to outrun a bevy of Texas linesmen, got a little help and was away down the sideline except for Billy Pyle, the Texas safety.

Paul Page blocked Pyle and it was Walker in a walk.

When he converted, Texas was beat, but it took a long time and a flock of heartbreaking events to spell out the first defeat in 17 games for Texas on its home field. It was the first SMU victory here in eight years.

Texas took the kickoff and bowled 69 yards to the SMU 11-yard line. From there, Ray Borneman blew off tackle for what would have been a first down on the 6-yard line, but here fate struck the first of a series of devastating blows to the Orange.

The play was called back because the Longhorns had been a split-second too slow in getting the play started. The penalty was destined to be the only one of the afternoon against Texas, but it couldn't have come at a better time for SMU.

With fourth-and-9 from the 16, Paul Campbell threw a pass that (like two later ones) was too high and too long beyond the end line.

The Steers still had the stuff to drive back to the SMU 16-yard line in the quarter, and roll 68 yards on 13 plays to score early in the second, but that first failure unques-

GAME 7 SMU VS. TEXAS, 1948

tionably took a lot our of the Long-horns.

Randall Clay, who had made 10 of 11 extra points, missed after Borneman had blasted for the last foot of the touchdown drive and that was the second nail in the Texas coffin.

If you will excuse us for doubling back, we'd like to mention here that Walker, in spite of his brilliant over-all performance, lost 2 more yards than the meager 3 he gained on eight running plays after his touchdown gallop.

The point is made to call attention to the peculiar course of events of the day.

Perhaps the big plays of the partly cloudy afternoon occurred a few min-utes after Clay's astonishing miss. Texas was on the offense again. Pyle had inter-cepted a pass by Gilbert Johnson and Texas had the ball on the Mustang 34.

On an attempted hand off, there was a foul-up in the Texas backfield and the ball bounced on the fly from Campbell's hands into the arms of tackle Joe Etheridge of SMU.

That set up SMU's second touch-down. On eight plays (three passes from Johnson to Raleigh Blakely for 11, 8 and 9 yards) the Mustangs scored.

The aerials carried to the Texas 3-yard line. Walker then carried three times for 1 yard on each try for the touchdown.

The Longhorns made several big plays against SMU but only scored once.

Texas was eight points down and all but out. The half ended on that 14-6 score.

Texas received the kickoff that opened the third quar-ter and had hammered its way past midfield when Campbell was knocked loose from the ball on a pass attempt and Gene Roberds, a guard, recovered for SMU on the Texas 34.

The Mustangs didn't score on the following series but, Walker punted out on the Texas 45-yard line and the Steers were in a hole from which they couldn't escape, in spite of a great 53-yard quick kick by Borneman.

With Johnson pitching to Walker, Zohn Milam, Kyle Rote and Walker again, the Mustangs went to a first down on the Texas 26. Gene Roberts ripped off 7 on a tricky

143

reverse and added one more on an end run.

With third-and-1 on the 18-yard line, Walker passed quick and short to Blakely for 5 yards on the first half of a play that had Rote running just back of Blakely.

The big SMU end practically batted the ball to the San Antonio flyer, who raced 13 yards for the touchdown.

Walker converted, but SMU was penalized 15 yards for holding and Walker repeated, this time from placement on the 25-yard line.

Doak rams into the heart of the Texas defense for a TD.

That was all the scoring. SMU had gone 70 yards on three plays, 34 on eight, and 59 on 11 for three touchdowns.

Texas had gone 68 on 13 for its one touchdown, missed on moves of 69, 22, 31, 55 and 62 yards, the latter two coming after the final score.

Next to Walker, Johnson was the mainspring in the SMU offense. He did nothing except pass, but he completed 10 of 17 for 89 yards.

The SMU line did nothing startling on offense and gave up a lot of yards, but Brownie Lewis, Fred Goodwin and John Hamberger stood out on defense. The

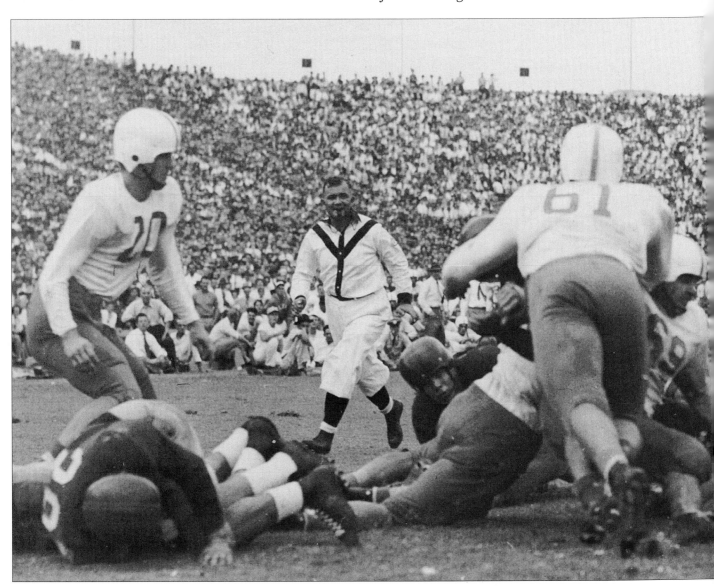

GAME 7 SMU VS. TEXAS, 1948

linebacking work of fullback David Moon, though, did more toward quieting the Steers than the work of any linesman.

The really important contribution by SMU linemen was the fumble recoveries by Ethridge and Roberds. They were really big plays.

Dick Harris was a standout on offense and defense for Texas. Vasicek and George Petrovich also did exceptionally well as the entire Texas line outcharged their rival forwards.

Borneman and Clay were the biggest Texas running backs, rushing for 99 and 95 yards respectively, but Paul

Campbell, despite some mishaps, was still the best Texas back on the field.

He called a good game, handled the ball well and completed 9 of 17 passes for 115 yards.

He just wasn't good enough to withstand the Mustangs and the errorless game they played.

SCORE BY PERIODS

SMU	7	7	7	0 —	21
Texas	0	6	0	0 —	6

SMU Weathers Webfoot Rally, 21-13

Fort-Worth Star-Telegram

DALLAS, Jan. 1, 1949

Professor Madison Bell and his sterling troop of SMU city slickers put on a smooth and profitable performance for the honest but too trusting folk from Oregon on Saturday afternoon.

Trotting out all their favorite feats of legerdemain — including the flicker play, the "cruncher" and the double-double reverse — the fast-talking Southwest Conference champions unloaded a carload of their favorite pain-killers on the unsuspecting visitors before they could bellow "Hey Rube!"

While Doak Walker banged the drum and that outstanding new performer named Kyle Rote tinkled the tambourine, the smart red shirts sold the gap-mouthed boys of Oregon University a 21-13 defeat in the 13th Cotton Bowl.

Some 69,000 fans attended, and departed convinced that the Oregonians are the solid, well-coached team that deserved the co-championship of the Pacific Coast Conference.

But compared to the suave, frock-coated Methodists, the West Coast team lacked imagination.

Sticking very close to straight T-formation, the Webfoots did the expected things in the expected way. They showed a fine passer in Norman Van Brocklin, but they were sadly lacking in receivers.

Van Brocklin's catchers had more passed balls than all

GAME 8 SMU vs. Oregon, 1949 Cotton Bowl

Dick Wilkins scored Oregon's first TD on a 23-yard reception in the end zone.

Doak blasts through a pair of Oregon defenders en route to the Ducks' goal line.

the backstops in the Texas League last season.

In sharp contrast, the Ponies returned to the scalpel-keen play that characterized their early games in the Southwest Conference. All of Rusty Russell's old stand-bys worked beautifully, and he had even added a few that had the addicts gasping.

You can sum the whole thing up by reporting that the Methodists were just too smooth, too urban and too skill-ful for the enemy.

The game wasn't even as close as the score would indi-cate. SMU had command from the kickoff and Oregon hardly hit a lick until they were 14 points down. As a mat-ter of fact, there wasn't much suspense in the proceedings.

Doak Walker wasn't the game's bright star. That hon-or went to Rote, the agile powerhouse who has two more full seasons to plague Southwest Conference foes. Rote was the trigger man Saturday.

His running was great and his receiving greater. Walker contributed plenty, especially in selection of plays. But it was a Rote day.

Strangely enough, Gilbert Johnson didn't figure much in the counting. The siege gun threw the ball well dur-ing the short time he played, but he really wasn't needed.

The suggestion of what was to come happened imme-diately. The Ponies took the kick and bucked the breeze and Oregon back 59 yards in 11 plays for the opening score.

Top plays were a long first down by Rote on the "cruncher play" — a trap of the Oregon right tackle — and Paul Page's 16-yard gallop on the old flicker. The most important play, though, occurred on fourth down on the Oregon 25. It was a hook pass from Walker to Raleigh Blakely for a first down on the 13.

Rote roared around end to the 2, Walker banged to the 1 and then slid through tackle five paces into the end zone.

There was one interesting aspect. The expected supe-riority of the Webfoot line, which had a 10-pound weight advantage, turned out to be a myth. The Pony forward just about held their own in all departments despite the fact that with center Fred Goodwin out because of a bad knee, Matty used Jim Marion, a little-known sophomore back, to work with Dave Moon on defense behind the line.

SMU used a variety of defenses, as usual, but the most effective was a four-three with two of the linebackers almost standing in the line. It held the hard-driving Ore-gon backs to 145 rushing yards.

Oregon was also fancy on defense, but employed a five-man setup most of the time. It too was fairly effec-tive against the run, but not versatile enough to bog down the varied Pony attack, especially in the clutches.

Incidentally, as expected, Oregon had the better pass-ing game. They gained 242 yards passing to 226 and 145 yards running to 111.

Walker also added an extra point to make it 7-0 after

GAME 8 SMU vs. Oregon, 1949 Cotton Bowl

five minutes of play.

Oregon fans were just waiting for their side to get to bat, but it was no go. The shifting Pony defense held the T-formation in check, and SMU kept moving. Another 45-yard drive moved to the Oregon 28 before an interception killed the threat.

SMU missed a fine chance late in the second period when a fumble set them up only 37 yards from the end zone. But a passing flurry by Johnson and hard running by Rote stalled on the Duck 11.

Oregon made its best move of the half just before the gun, reaching the Pony 39.

As an interesting sideline and indication of how SMU used brain instead of brawn, the Webfoots never quick-kicked with the stiff wind.

Doak breaks loose in the Oregon secondary.

SMU did it twice in the second quarter. One by Walker traveled 79 yards and rolled out right at the flag. The other by Rote went 84 yards to the Duck 12. They gave SMU a punting average of 82.5 yards in the first half.

Starting the third quarter, SMU quickly put the game in the cold box. They romped 80 yards on 10 plays after the kickoff — again into the wind — to make it 14-0.

Top plays were a wide reverse by Page and a double reverse that carried to the Duck 40. From the Oregon 35, Rote scored on a familiar-looking play.

It was from double wing, a trap from the outside on the Duck left guard, Rote broke into the clear and outran everyone.

Lindy Berry of TCU scored on the Ponies with a similar maneuver in the last game of the regular season.

With the game practically salted away, the Mustangs relaxed. The Ducks put on their first real thrust, a 63-yard march featuring straight run plays, that died on the SMU 5.

Early in the fourth quarter, Oregon finally tallied. They moved 53 yards on six plays, three of them fine passes from Van Brocklin.

One carried to the SMU 38 and another, to end Dick Wilkins, made it to the 23. From there, the same Wikins outmaneuvered Dick McKissack in the end zone, and took a Van Brocklin bullet for the score. The extra point was missed.

With an eight-point led, SMU looked safe enough, but they wanted more. They took the kickoff and paraded 66 yards in seven plays.

The top play was Rote's great catch of Walker's pass on the Duck 20. From the 3, Walker drove for what looked like a score, but SMU was offside. From the 8, little Gene Roberds started wide to the right, but back through tackle like a streak, and wasn't touched. Joe Ethridge kicked the extra point to make it 21-6.

With that lead, Matty and Rusty began to feed in their subs. Oregon then scored again, going 67 yards on eight plays.

The payoff was a pass from Van Brocklin that Darrell Robinson carried to the Pony 9. Three line smashes made the distance and point was good.

Just to prove they weren't messing around, SMU drove with the next kickoff all the way to the Duck 15, but Johnson's passes failed to make the final counter. It made no difference.

SCORE BY PERIODS

SMU	7	0	7	7	—	21
Oregon	0	0	0	13	—	13

Walker Leads SMU Past Mizzou

By Jack Murphy

Fort-Worth Star-Telegram

....

DALLAS, Oct. 1, 1949

Doak Walker and the dazzling Ponies of Southern Methodist whirled the Missouri Tigers around and around here Saturday night before 58,000 delighted partisans in a 28-27 victory that was far more decisive than the score would indicate.

With Walker personally scoring 22 points on three touchdowns and four extra points, the Ponies were in actual jeopardy only in the first quarter, when Missouri drove to a 7-0 lead on its first possession.

Unperturbed, Walker led the super-smooth Ponies to a 14-7 advantage at intermission and made the outcome almost certain by shooting ahead 28-14 after four minutes of the fourth quarter.

Missouri, in the tradition of its 35-34 defeat of Ohio State last week, made it respectable in the final five minutes, but an SMU victory was already a foregone conclusion.

The game's actual breaking point occurred after 14:40 of the final quarter, when SMU guard Jack Halliday smashed in to block John Glorioso's attempted extra point. That reduced the Pony lead to 28-20, and, in light of what developed in the final minute, was the difference in the game.

It was realization of the year-long SMU dream of

GAME 9 SMU vs. Missouri, 1949

Doak and Kyle Rote (44) were a potent duo for the Mustangs in 1948 and '49. Against Missouri they rushed for 202 yards.

avenging the only defeat on its 1948 record. The South-west Conference champions had gone undefeated in 16 straight games when Don Farout's split-T Tigers surprised them, 20-14, last year at Columbia.

This time, the Ponies answered the question that bobs up with every game. How much do they miss Gilbert Johnson?

For this one night, at least, they didn't need old No. 45 at all. In fact, they didn't bother much with passing.

While the glossy Ponies glided for 14 first downs and 284 yards on the ground, they threw only eight passes, completing four for 66 yards. Walker threw seven of that

number and accounted for all of the completions.

But the Doaker was deadly effective on the ground. He carried 29 times for a 129 yards and would have done better but for a 17-yard loss on a pass that backfired.

His running mate, Kyle Rote, ground for 73 yards on 18 carries, Frank Payne went 52 on 11 and sophomore Henry Stollenwerck of Waxahachie made 27 on five.

Walker plunged 3 yards for the first SMU touchdown, bucked over from the 1 for the third, and dashed 19 yards around end for the finale in the last quarter.

Missouri stunned the Ponies right at the outset when

halfback Dick Braznell took the opening kickoff in the end zone and raced to the Tiger 45. Ten plays later, the Tigers went ahead, 7-0, when Phil Klein sneaked over from the SMU 1 and John Glorioso converted.

After fizzling on the Tiger 25 on an earlier bid, the Ponies struck back after 7½ minutes of the second quarter for a 7-7 tie. Using nothing but running plays, SMU marched 82 yards on 20 plays.

In the series, Walker carried nine times and accounted for 42 yards — exactly half the distance covered. This included his short scoring burst from the Tiger 3-yard line.

Rote was the other big gainer on the drive, stepping off 30 yards on seven attempts.

It was McKissack who kept it going, though, diving (literally) over tackle for a vital first down on the Tiger 24 on a fourth-down try.

A break in the guise of a fumble recovery by linebacker L.D. Russell, a standout all evening, set up the Ponies' second touchdown and sent them ahead, 14-7. Russell, a replacement for the departed Dave Moon, jumped on a Bob Henley fumble on the Tiger 28, and eight plays later SMU had a touchdown.

With exactly five minutes remaining in the first half, Rote spurted 8 yards around right end to the end zone, knocking over the corner flag as he went in. Walker converted again and it was SMU 14, Missouri 7.

The Ponies wasted no time at all as they jumped ahead, 21-7, in the third quarter.

First, it was a 10-play drive that covered 68 yards, Walker going over right tackle for the last step. Walker set it up with a 20-yard dash and then a pass to Rote was good for 24 yards to the Tiger 16.

Zohn Milam showed up on the old end around a moment later, racing to the Tiger 3 before being pushed out of bounds by Glorioso. Walker dived to the 1 and then hit right tackle for the score. Converting again, he sent the Mustangs ahead, 21-7, after only four minutes.

Missouri struck back on the ensuing kickoff after Braznell returned to the Tiger 25. In 10 plays, the Tigers traveled 75 yards, with Braznell going over from the 3 on a pitchout.

Braznell and Glorioso figured in the drive's two key moves. First, Braznell threw a running southpaw pass good for 30 yards to Glorioso on the SMU 18. Then the procedure was reverse, Glorioso pitching to Braznell on the 4.

The pass was incomplete but officials ruled that Pony end Bobby Folsom had interfered with Braznell and the Tigers set up in business on the 4. Two plays made 1 yard and then Braznell went wide on a pitchout for Missouri's second touchdown. When Glorioso converted, it was SMU 21, Missouri 14.

SMU then got away for its winning counter after Klein kicked out of bounds on the Pony 49. Two Rote rushes and a roughing penalty pushed the Tigers back to their 28 and SMU was under way.

Payne, Walker and Rote carried to the 19 and then Walker went all the way on an unusual play that developed at left tackle.

Apparently checked at the line of scrimmage, Walker suddenly spurted to the outside and raced across without being touched.

Walker converted and SMU led, 28-14, with 11:15 to play in the final quarter.

Missouri came back with a 12-play, 72-yard drive to make it 28-20. Upback Martin Sauer shot a jump pass to end Gene Ackerman for the last yard. The game was lost here, though, when Halliday put an arm in front of Glorioso's placement attempt.

The final Tiger touchdown was delivered with only 20 seconds showing on the clock. It was an 80-yard effort that needed 14 plays and was climaxed with Henley passing to Ackerman in the end zone from the SMU 3.

Glorioso converted and time remained for only one play after McKissack returned to the SMU 40. The churning Pony fullback was perfectly content to take a 5-yard loss as the gun sounded.

SCORE BY PERIODS

Missouri	7	0	7	13	—	27
SMU	0	14	7	7	—	28

Walker & Co. Rout Hogs, 34-6

BY JACK MURPHY
Fort-Worth Star-Telegram

DALLAS, Nov. 12, 1949

A purposeful Southern Methodist football team — with Doak Walker again riding the high road to all-America eminence — gorged itself on some particularly succulent pork here this chill blustery afternoon before 42,000 onlookers in the Cotton Bowl. With Walker, the master chef, wielding a knife that cut Arkansas Razorbacks to shreds in the opening quarter, the defending Southwest Conference champions rolled to a ridiculously easy 34-6 triumph.

Walker was three horses and a man bundled into one compact frame as he squirted through Arkansas' sturdy line for three touchdowns, tossed a touchdown pass to Johnny Champion good for 54 yards, and kicked three points from placement.

The Ponies this day were the champions of 1947 and 1948 as they dusted off a good, sound Arkansas team that can be dangerous at any time. They were in command almost from the opening kickoff; they never made a serious error and almost everything worked for them.

Walker & Co. marched 39 yards on six plays for a 6-0 lead the second time they handled the ball, then rushed over two more counters in the last five minutes of the first quarter.

That startling outburst gave the Mustangs a 20-0 advantage and put the decision in deep freeze.

A scoreless second quarter followed, the two teams exchanged touchdowns in the third, and young Fred Benners came along in the closing chap-

MIGHTY MUSTANGS of 1945, '47, '48 & '49 WHO HELPED DOAK WALKER BECOME 3-TIME CONSENSUS ALL-AMERICA

A TOAST TO DOAK WALKER

ter to provide the final Pony tally.

Though this was no one-man achievement, the brilliant Walker, once again sound physically, clearly was the all-America back he has been proclaimed for three seasons.

He took a fearful drubbing on occasion while pounding the guards and tackles, but dazzling Walker squeezed through his openings for 98 yards on 18 carries and completed four of five passes for 113 paces.

One of his aerial strikes (to Champion in the opening period) was a prodigious thing that traveled 39 yards on the fly and brought on a touchdown play that covered 54 yards in all.

As expected, the Ponies bottled up Arkansas' prayerful passing game, but the victory for their defense came

against the Porker ground game. Barring one lapse (when Gino Mazzanti charged 45 yards in the fourth) the Mustang forwards reared up and threw back almost everything that came toward them.

This superiority was best evidenced in the first half when SMU was striking for a margin of safety. Arkansas crossed midfield only three times, reaching the Mustang 36, 34 and 44. The last time the Hogs were helped by a 15-yard penalty.

The Razorback attack again was bereft of most of its striking power. Leon (Muscles) Campbell squirmed and sweated through the long (for him) afternoon, still unable to play because of a knee injury.

In the first two periods Arkansas didn't complete a pass (five attempted) and made only 49 yards aground.

"Walker slithered over a mass of humans at right guard for a touchdown on the next play."

Jack Murphy

By contrast, SMU moved for a total of 204 yards, picking up 102 yards rushing and the same number over head.

The first Methodist touchdown came after a short kick by Louie Shaufele, Arkansas fullback, the ball going out on the Porker 39.

On second down, Walker fired a pass to end Raleigh Blakely in the fight flat, Blakely shaking off two defenders at the 30 and racing to the 19. Thrown back to the 27 on another passing attempt, Walker connected with Zohn Milam on the 17, and the big Pony end charged to the one-foot line before being pushed out of bounds.

Walker slithered over a mass of humans at right guard for a touchdown on the next play. His try for point was declared no good.

Two minutes later the Ponies had a 13-0 lead. Starting from the Porker 45 after another short punt into the wind, Walker started to his right as though to attempt a pass.

But he suddenly handed the ball to wingback Kyle Rote, who was headed the opposite direction.

With only one blocker, Rote sprinted 34 yards to the Arkansas 11 before going beyond the boundary. Walker sent Dick McKissack into left guard for a yard and then sent Dick McKissack into left guard for a yard and then took personal charge. Cutting quickly over right guard, he feinted a linebacker out of position and then hurled himself between two defenders

at the 1.

Walker kicked the point-after and it was 13-0 with 2:59 to play in the first period.

It was Walker and a football again in the period's last minute. Standing on the Porker 46, he took his time until he spotted Champion behind two defenders on the 15. Then he reared back a la Dizzy Dean, and let go a high wobbly toss that Champion snatched while off balance.

Champion, quickly regaining his footing, raced into the end zone without being touched. Walker converted a second time and SMU led, 20-0, with 16 seconds remaining in the quarter.

After a scoreless second period, Arkansas elected to utilize a brisk wind blowing from the north and quickly struck for its only touchdown. Mazzanti, Ray Parks and Alvin Duck were the steady gainers as the Porkers moved 058 yards in eight plays.

Parks took it over right tackle, spinning across from the 4 after being momentarily checked. Duval Thornton's extra-point kick was awry.

This came after five minutes of the third period and revived Arkansas' flickering hopes until Walker went to work again.

Here, he sparked a 71-yard effort that needed 12 plays. Carrying five times in the series, Walker gained 40 yards, including his bolt across the goal from the Porker 3. Doak again kicked goal and SMU led, 27-6, after 12 minutes.

After Mazzanti had raced 45 yards on a delayed buck to the SMU 9 only to see the ball go on over on downs four plays later on the SMU 5, SMU racked up its fifth and last touchdown in the fourth quarter.

Benners was in charge and he needed only three passes from the Porker 44. The last was a pitch to end Charley Russell that covered 26 yards. Only 1:26 remained when Bill Sullivan kicked the extra point.

SCORE BY PERIODS

Arkansas	0	0	6	0	—	6
SMU	20	0	7	7	—	34

BIOGRAPHIES

ABOUT THE AUTHOR

Whit Canning is a sports writer with the *Fort Worth Star-Telegram*, where he has covered Southwest Conference and WAC football. He previously worked with the *Fort Worth Press*, covering the Southwest Conference and the Dallas Cowboys.

He is also the author of *Sam Baugh: Best There Ever Was.*

A native of Fort Worth and a graduate of Texas Christian University, this is his second book.

ABOUT THE EDITOR

Dan Jenkins is one of America's most renowned sports writers. Jenkins is the author of more than a dozen books, including the bestsellers, *Semi-Tough* (1972), *Dead Solid Perfect* (1974), *Limo* (1976), *Baja Oklahoma* (1981), *Life It's Own Self* (1984), *Fast Copy* (1988), and *You Gotta Play Hurt* (1991).

Jenkins is also the editor of *Greatest Moments in TCU Football History, Sam Baugh: Best There Ever Was, Darrell Royal: Dance With Who Brung Ya* and *John David Crow: Heart of a Champion.*

A native of Fort Worth and an alumnus of TCU, Jenkins' most enjoyable boyhood memories are having watched Sam Baugh and Davey O'Brien lead the Horned Frogs to national championships in 1935 and 1938.

CAREER STATS

At SMU

Year	RUSHING				PASSING				PUNTING	
	G	Att.	Yards	Avg.	Att.	Comp.	Yards	TD's	No.	Avg.
1945	5	68	289	4.3	65	38	387	5	11	31.3
1947	11	181	740	4.1	60	34	411	12	15	33.0
1948	11	122	598	4.9	56	32	383	12	36	44.0
1949	8	130	449	3.6	58	35	605	11	23	41.7
Totals	35	501	2,076	4.1	239	139	1,786	40	85	39.6

At Detroit Lions

Year	RUSHING					RECEIVING				PUNTING		
	G	Att.	Yards	Avg.	TD's	Rec.	Yards	Avg.	TD's	No.	Yards	Avg.
1950	12	83	386	4.7	5	35	534	15.3	6	32	1,278	39.9
1951	12	79	356	4.5	2	22	421	19.1	4	9	316	35.1
1952	7	26	106	4.1	0	11	90	8.2	0	0	0	0.0
1953	12	66	337	5.1	2	30	502	16.7	3	0	0	0.0
1954	12	32	240	7.5	1	32	564	17.6	3	0	0	0.0
1955	12	23	95	4.1	2	22	428	19.5	5	9	362	40.2
Totals	67	309	1,520	4.9	12	152	2,539	16.7	21	50	1,956	39.1

CREDITS

Bettmann Archives — 66, 108, 134-135, 148.

Cotton Bowl — 14.

Center for American History, The University of Texas — 64, 143, 144-145.

DeGolyer Library, Southern Methodist University — Back Cover (*Collier's*-both, *Sport* and *Look* covers), 84.

Fort Worth Star-Telegram Collection, University of Texas at Arlington Archives — Front Cover, iv, x, 18, 23, 25, 36, 38, 40-41, 54, 59, 81, 90, 102, 109, 111, 121, 126, 127, 138-139.

Dan Jenkins Collection — 21, 98-99.

SMU Sports Information — iii, xii-xiii, 19, 43, 46-47, 70, 83, 92, 118-119, 123, 128, 132-133, 142, 151, 154.

The Collection of the Texas/Dallas History and Archives, Dallas Public Library — 16-17, 33, 107, 141.

Time Inc. — Back Cover (*Life* cover), 22, 45, 52, 75.

Doak Walker Collection — vi, viii-ix, xi, 14-15, 26, 29, 30, 32, 34-35, 37, 48, 56, 61, 65, 69, 79, 104-105, 113, 114, 115, 116, 117, 131, 149.

Wide World Photo — 110.